TOXIC GENEROSITY

BY AMY LAW

Published by Kududa

ISBN: 979-8-9914171-0-5

TOXIC GENEROSITY

BY AMY LAW

TABLE OF CONTENTS

INTRODUCTION

On the surface, it fosters connection, goodwill, and the promise of a cohesive society. It can uplift spirits, strengthen bonds, and create lasting connections. Yet, beneath its idealized image lies a complex interplay of motives, societal expectations, and unintended consequences that warrant deeper examination. This complexity is what makes the study of generosity so fascinating and worthy of exploration.

What if generosity isn't always as pure as it appears? Beneath its seemingly straightforward nature lies a world of hidden motivations, unspoken desires, and deeply ingrained emotional wound patterns that influence how generosity is expressed and experienced. Generosity is far from simple; it is a multifaceted trait shaped by psychological, societal, and relational factors. What truly drives someone to give? Is it an act of unconditional kindness, or does it mask a need for validation, control, or belonging? Humans, by nature, do not act without reason—a motive guides every action. It is the motive that differentiates healthy generosity from pathological generosity.

This book, *Toxic Generosity*, offers a unique perspective by challenging the conventional narrative of generosity. It explores the hidden pitfalls of generosity, from societal pressures that glorify self-sacrifice to the ego-driven need for recognition. Generosity, it argues, is often entangled with complexities that distort its true essence. Acts of giving can be beautiful, but they can also come at a cost—emotional burnout, strained relationships, or unintended consequences that leave both giver and receiver feeling trapped.

What if the urge to give arises from unresolved childhood wounds, experiences of injustice, unconscious idealism, or a deep longing to fill an emotional void? What happens when giving is motivated by cultural pressure, religious beliefs, or the pursuit of power disguised as altruism? How does family influence how people learn to give—or, sometimes, over-give? While often well-intentioned, these influences can sometimes lead to unintended consequences, making it crucial to explore their profound impacts on both the giver and receiver.

This book invites a critical reassessment of the role of generosity in society. It uncovers the less-explored side of generosity, encouraging introspection and asking: Is generosity genuinely selfless, or are hidden needs driving it? When does giving bring fulfillment, and when does it lead to resentment or imbalance in relationships? How can a form of giving be cultivated those nurtures both the giver and the receiver? The ultimate goal is to foster healthier, more authentic relationships through a balanced understanding of generosity. *Toxic Generosity book* helps untangle generosity from guilt, societal expectations, and ego, fostering a more authentic, balanced approach to this revered virtue. By exploring the cultural, religious, and psychological dimensions of generosity, the book provides a rich and multifaceted understanding of this complex human trait. The goal is not to judge generosity but to understand its true essence, and in doing so, to stimulate intellectual curiosity and engagement.

Generosity is not inherently virtuous or harmful, it is what is made of it. Through introspective analysis and real-world examples, the book explores the unspoken pains generosity can carry and its transformative power when practiced with balance and intention. This journey into the hidden layers of giving and the nuances of altruism aims to create a culture of generosity that uplifts both the giver and the receiver, fostering healthier, more authentic relationships.

This book is not just about giving; it is about the givers and receivers. It delves into what generosity reveals about the human heart, the deep emotional currents that drive individuals, and how generosity can be consciously shaped to have a positive impact. This exploration of generosity's hidden layers may change how the world's generosity is understood and practiced.

UNDERSTANDING GENEROSITY: THE NATURE OF GIVING

Generosity, at its core, is one of humanity's most celebrated virtues. It embodies the act of willingly giving something of value—whether it bo time, resources, or emotional support—to another without expectation of direct reciprocation. On the surface, generosity fosters connection, goodwill, and the promise of a cohesive society. Yet, like many human traits, it is not without complexity. Understanding generosity requires examining not just its external acts but the deeper psychological, societal, and relational layers it carries.

THE PARADOX OF GENEROSITY

Generosity presents a paradox: it can be both an expression of abundance and a potential source of depletion. At its best, generosity fosters connection, strengthens relationships, and uplifts both the giver and the receiver. However, an imbalance can lead to dependency, resentment, or even manipulation. This duality of generosity—its capacity to be both beneficial and harmful—is a fascinating aspect that deserves exploration to truly understand its meaning.

At one end of the spectrum, generosity stems from genuine care and empathy, reflecting a sincere desire to support and uplift others without expecting anything in return. In such cases, both the giver and the receiver benefit; the giver experiences fulfillment and purpose, while the receiver feels valued and supported. This form of generosity nurtures relationships and promotes mutual respect.

Additionally, reciprocity—the act of giving back—can also be a form of generosity. When the recipient of a generous act acknowledges and appreciates the gift, it creates a positive cycle of giving and receiving, further strengthening the relationship.

However, generosity is not always as straightforward or virtuous as it appears. Psychological, societal, and relational factors shape it, making it susceptible to hidden motivations. For instance, guilt over past actions, the need for validation from others, or an unconscious desire for power and control can influence acts of giving. Some individuals may give out of obligation, fear of judgment, or as a means of seeking approval. Others might use generosity as a tool for influencing, creating a sense of indebtedness, asserting dominance, or subtly manipulating the recipient.

When generosity becomes transactional or stems from unexamined motives, it risks disrupting the balance in relationships. Instead of fostering goodwill, it can breed dependency, entitlement, or resentment. A giver who consistently overextends themselves may eventually feel unappreciated, while a receiver who becomes accustomed to generosity may develop expectations without reciprocity. In extreme cases, hidden resentment can emerge, leading to acts of betrayal that erode trust and damage the very relationships generosity was meant to strengthen.

This complexity underscores the importance of self-awareness in acts of giving. True generosity respects the needs and boundaries of both parties. It is not a zero-sum game but a dynamic process requiring mindfulness, balance, and intentionality. Recognizing our motivations and setting healthy boundaries can ensure that generosity remains an enriching force rather than a source of emotional strain, empowering us to maintain control over our actions.

Ultimately, generosity is neither inherently virtuous nor harmful; it becomes what we make of it. By examining our intentions and the underlying dynamics of giving, we can cultivate a more authentic and sustainable approach. This awareness allows us to nurture a culture of generosity that benefits both the giver and the receiver, ensuring its impact remains positive, empowering, and enduring.

PSYCHOLOGICAL BENEFITS AND COMPLEXITIES

Acts of generosity are not just about giving,
they are about receiving too. The giver often

experiences a profound sense of joy, improved well-being, and heightened self-esteem. Studies have shown that giving activates the brain's reward system, releasing chemicals like dopamine and oxytocin, which create a sense of happiness and satisfaction. This phenomenon, often referred to as the "helper's high," not only benefits the recipients but also brings a deep sense of fulfillment to the givers.

When people give, they feel a sense of internal happiness, and their relationships with others deepen, strengthening their sense of belonging and appreciation. This psychological response is highly motivating, as it allows the giver to feel good about themselves while simultaneously fostering stronger emotional connections with others, deepening the shared sense of humanity. Therefore, generosity becomes more than just a charitable act; it becomes an emotional and psychological growth experience for the giver.

However, this psychological reward can create a paradox. The more someone gives to feel good, the more they may feel compelled to continue, even when it becomes unsustainable or detrimental. Initially, this giving may be driven by a genuine desire to help others, but over time, it can become linked to the pursuit of emotional rewards. This compulsion can blur the line between healthy generosity and over-giving, potentially leading to emotional exhaustion or feelings of inadequacy when the expected emotional rewards do not materialize. It's important to be aware of these potential negative effects of over-giving to maintain a healthy balance in generosity.

When a person over-gives, they may experience burnout. Despite generosity being inherently positive, continuous giving without boundaries can lead to exhaustion. Additionally, when the receiver starts taking generosity for granted, it can result in feelings of underappreciation or disappointment for the giver, creating an emotional disconnect. In these cases, what once was a generous act may transform into a source of tension rather than connection, and the relationship can suffer as a result. This transformation of a generous act into a source of tension illustrates the potential consequences of over-giving. This psychological complexity emphasizes the importance of maintaining balance in acts of generosity. Generosity should be driven by genuine care and a willingness to share, not by the need for ongoing emotional gratification. Over time, giving without self-awareness can lead to burnout and resentment. Sustainable generosity requires being mindful of one's own emotional needs and ensuring that giving is not done at the cost of the giver's well-being. This stress on the importance of maintaining balance in acts of generosity underlines the need for self-awareness and emotional regulation.

SOCIETAL ROLE OF GENEROSITY

Generosity, personal virtue, and a pillar that holds together the social fabric of communities, families, and societies at large, has a rich historical significance. From ancient tribal customs of communal sharing to modern-day philanthropic endeavors, generosity has been pivotal in creating and sustaining bonds among individuals. Its role goes beyond simply giving—it is the social glue that fosters cooperation, mutual aid, and trust. In many cultures, generosity is not just a personal choice, but a moral obligation, a sign of good character, or an essential duty tied to one's social identity and status. In these societies, giving is seen as a reflection of one's integrity, humanity, and worth.

From the early days of human civilization, when individuals shared resources to ensure group survival, to the modern concepts of charity and philanthropy, generosity has been central to social cohesion. Through these acts of kindness and sharing, communities are built, and social bonds are strengthened. Within this framework, generosity encourages a sense of mutual responsibility and collective well-being, creating a balanced relationship between giving and receiving, ensuring everyone's needs are met.

However, the societal view of generosity is not without its complexities. While often celebrated as a virtue, cultural norms and societal expectations can pressure individuals to give beyond their capacity, driven by the desire for acceptance and the belief that pleasing others or fulfilling certain expectations will lead to being loved by God. This pressure can lead people to overextend themselves financially, emotionally, physically, or energetically to meet these demands.

The moral imperative to be generous can sometimes lead individuals to prioritize the needs of others over their own, creating a significant emotional and physical toll. Whether it is the expectations set by religious teachings, family traditions, or societal values, the emphasis on giving can sometimes cause individuals to feel as though they are obligated to provide, even when doing so may be detrimental to their well-being.

The pressure to give can be especially intense in families where close-knit bonds and shared responsibilities are central. Cultural expectations often dictate that generosity is not just a choice but a duty, and individuals may feel a deep sense of responsibility to support loved ones, regardless of their personal limitations. This expectation can be particularly overwhelming when the giver feels they are not receiving the same level of support or acknowledgment in return, leading to an imbalance in relationships. Over time, this can cause the giver to experience resentment, exhaustion, or emotional burnout as their needs go unmet in favor of continually giving to others. It's important to acknowledge these pressures and their potential impact on individuals.

The societal elevation of generosity can sometimes obscure its more complicated realities. The constant drive to give can become a source of stress rather than fulfillment. In this context, generosity can become entangled with feelings of obligation, making it less of an altruistic act and more of a burden. This imbalance can disrupt personal well-being and strain relationships, turning what was meant to be a nurturing, selfless act into a source of tension or resentment.

It is essential, therefore, to acknowledge the nuanced nature of generosity in a societal context. While generosity can be a powerful force for good, it must be practiced in balance. Understanding that generosity is not always about self-sacrifice is key to ensuring it remains a healthy and positive force within relationships and communities. This means recognizing when giving becomes excessive or when it is no longer sustainable, both for the giver and the receiver. Instead, the focus should be on mindful, conscious acts of generosity. This could involve setting clear boundaries, communicating openly about needs and limitations, and ensuring that both parties feel valued and respected in the exchange. These practices can help nurture both the giver and the receiver, ensuring the social bond remains strong and mutually beneficial.

In conclusion, while generosity plays a crucial role in fostering trust, cooperation, and community, it must be approached with awareness of its potentlal emotional and social complexities. It is not merely the act of giving that builds a strong society but the understanding of when and how to give to support both individual well-being and collective harmony. When practiced in a balanced and mindful way, generosity can lead to a sense of fulfillment, strengthen relationships, and contribute to a healthier, more harmonious society. The actual value of generosity lies in its ability to foster genuine connections without overburdening those who practice it, allowing it to remain a source of strength and cohesion within society.

THE INTERPERSONAL DYNAMICS OF GIVING

Though often celebrated as an altruistic and virtuous act, generosity is rarely a solitary experience. It is inherently relational, unfolding within the context of relationships where both the giver and the receiver play significant roles. Giving creates an intricate web of interactions shaped by the emotional, psychological, and social undercurrents that define the connection between the two parties. This relational aspect introduces complexities that go beyond simply exchanging goods, time, or energy.

At its essence, every act of giving builds a connection between two individuals. However, this connection is never neutral. It is imbued with expectations, assumptions, and emotional consequences that may not always be visible on the surface. The giver, for example, may experience a profound sense of fulfillment, validation, or even a sense of superiority from their generosity, which can be deeply rewarding. Meanwhile, the receiver may feel gratitude, indebtedness, or a sense of obligation. Whether acknowledged or not, these emotional responses carry significant weight in shaping the trajectory of the relationship.

One of the more delicate dynamics of generosity is the balance—or imbalance—it creates within the relationship. The act of giving, while seemingly straightforward, has the power to subtly but profoundly shift the relational dynamic. This is particularly true when one party consistently gives more than they receive—whether in material resources, emotional labor, time, or attention. Over time, such disparities can generate emotional tension that may not be immediately visible but is deeply felt, underscoring the importance of vigilance in maintaining balance.

For instance, when the giver consistently extends more than the receiver can match, an unspoken power imbalance can emerge. Even unintentionally, the giver may gain a position of influence or control in the relationship. On the other hand, the receiver may begin to feel indebted, as though they owe something in return, which can subtly shift the dynamics of equality and mutual respect.

When this imbalance goes unaddressed, trust may begin to erode. While the giver may feel good about their actions, they might unintentionally create an emotional strain or sense of power over the receiver. In contrast, the receiver could struggle with feelings of inadequacy, guilt, or resentment. The emotional burden may worsen if the receiver cannot reciprocate the generosity to the same extent. The weight of unfulfilled expectations can fester, leading to unspoken frustrations and, in some cases, an eventual breakdown in the relationship.

The emotional consequences of giving can be profound, especially when one party gives excessively without acknowledgment or reciprocation. In some instances, the giver may even feel victimized, as though they are giving too much without receiving enough in return. This can create a cycle of over-giving and emotional exhaustion, where the giver's needs are left unmet, and the relationship becomes unbalanced.

Emphasizing the role of balance in giving, it becomes clear that healthy relationships are not about one-sided acts, but about mutual respect, reciprocal energetic connection, and shared care. Both parties need to be attuned to the emotional dynamics and be able to identify when giving starts to create tension or imbalance. A balanced dynamic, rooted in respect, creates a nurturing environment where both parties feel valued and supported, ensuring that giving remains a positive force in the relationship.

Essentially, giving transcends the physical act and fosters a relationship rooted in mutual respect and empathy. It involves an acute awareness of the emotional and psychological dynamics at play. By maintaining balance, giving can enrich relationships, strengthen bonds, and create an environment where both the giver and the receiver feel deeply connected and understood.

THE FINE LINE BETWEEN HEALTHY AND UNHEALTHY GIVING

Healthy (conscious) and unhealthy (unconscious) generosity are shaped by intention and boundaries. When generosity comes from a place of awareness and clear limits, it enriches both the giver and the receiver. However, when it lacks intention or disregards personal boundaries, it can lead to harm, resentment, or imbalance in relationships.

Conscious generosity is grounded in authenticity and driven by a genuine desire to help others without seeking recognition or return. It remains pure when given freely—without pressure, manipulation, or the pursuit of power and self-gratification. Rooted in emotional and psychological well-being, this form of giving reflects a sincere commitment to kindness and meaningful connection.

Healthy generosity fosters a stronger bond between giver and receiver, expanding into a more profound sense of community where generosity becomes a tool for upliftment and empowerment. In many cases, the giver remains anonymous, offering their support in secrecy, which creates an unspoken connection that transcends personal recognition and physical presence. When practiced with balance and awareness, generosity becomes a source of empowerment rather than dependency, allowing both the giver and the receiver to grow without creating an unhealthy dynamic of obligation or reliance. This act of giving respects the autonomy and dignity of the receiver, allowing them to feel supported without diminishing their self-worth. The empowerment that healthy giving brings to both parties is a testament to its transformative power, inspiring us to embrace it in our relationships.

Unhealthy or unconscious generosity, on the other hand, often stems from unexamined motives, where a need for external validation or fear of social judgment drives the giver's actions. This form of giving is fueled by guilt, a desire for approval, or the fear of rejection. It is typically unsustainable, relying on external affirmation or social obligation rather than an internal desire to give. This type of generosity can lead to burnout for the giver, who may continue giving without considering their own needs or boundaries. Over time, this can breed resentment, especially if the receiver seems indifferent or ungrateful. Similarly, the receiver may start feeling that they are the giver's responsibility, creating a dependency that undermines their autonomy. Unhealthy generosity disrupts a relationship's natural flow of give-and-take, creating emotional strain for both the giver and the receiver. When generosity is not reciprocated or stems from an imbalanced place, it fosters a sense of exploitation and damages the relationship, ultimately diminishing the true spirit of generosity. This underscores the importance of reciprocity in generosity, promoting balance and fairness in relationships. Understanding and avoiding unhealthy generosity is crucial to preserving the health of our relationships.

The key to maintaining healthy generosity lies in the awareness of one's intentions and the establishment of clear boundaries. A generous act should be a conscious choice, made with a complete understanding of its impact on both the giver and the receiver. Healthy giving involves recognizing the limits of one's resources—whether those resources are time, energy, or financial—and ensuring that the giving does not come at the expense of one's well-being. Both the giver and the receiver need to be conscious of their roles in the exchange, ensuring that generosity fosters mutual respect, empowerment, and growth. When both parties recognize their needs and communicate openly, the act of giving remains a source of strength and connection rather than a breeding ground for dependency or resentment. Ultimately, the fine line between healthy and unhealthy generosity comes down to intention, awareness, and the recognition of boundaries. When generosity is grounded in authenticity and balanced by respect for autonomy, it becomes a powerful force for positive connection. However, when open generosity—where both the giver and receiver are known to each other—is driven by external pressures, unexamined motives, or a lack of boundaries, it can create strain and undermine the very qualities it seeks to promote. Therefore, understanding the dynamics of healthy versus unhealthy giving is crucial for maintaining relationships built on mutual respect, empowerment, and genuine connection.

GENEROSITY AND ITS RIPPLE EFFECTS

Generosity goes beyond simply giving; it creates significant ripples that influence social and relational dynamics. A generous act can inspire others, promoting a culture of kindness, empathy, and cooperation. It can strengthen relationships, build trust, and encourage a cycle of goodwill within communities. However, when generosity is motivated by obligation, control, or an unexamined need for validation, it can lead to unintended negative consequences, such as resentment, dependency, or imbalance.

Consider the case of a parent in a family dynamic who consistently over-gives. This well-intentioned action may unintentionally impede a child's ability to develop independence. Children who are not allowed to face challenges, make mistakes, and take responsibility may struggle to build resilience and essential life skills. Over time, this can create difficulties in navigating adulthood, as they may lack the confidence, problem-solving abilities, and emotional strength needed to succeed. Without understanding the effort, sacrifices, and decisions involved in achieving independence, they may repeatedly encounter failures in life, finding it hard to support themselves or cope with setbacks.

In friendships, it is essential to maintain a balanced approach to generosity. When one person consistently takes on the role of the giver—emotionally, financially, or in terms of effort—it can lead to unspoken expectations that create an imbalance. The giver may eventually feel drained or unappreciated, while the receiver might develop a sense of entitlement or dependency. In some cases, this dynamic can breed silent resentment, with the receiver harboring hidden frustration or even animosity toward the giver. This resentment can manifest in acts of betrayal, ultimately eroding trust and making the relationship unsustainable. To ensure a healthy and lasting friendship, both parties must give and receive in a way that fosters balance.

In professional settings, a culture that excessively emphasizes hard work, where employees feel compelled to always "go the extra mile" without boundaries, can lead to burnout. When hard work is expected continuously instead of being recognized, employees may feel undervalued, resulting in disengagement, decreased productivity, and high turnover rates. It is essential for organizations to acknowledge and appreciate their employees' efforts rather than expecting them to exceed their limits consistently.

On a larger scale, countries and societies that become overly reliant on handouts may struggle to achieve long-term success. Being on the receiving end for extended periods can create a false sense of security, discouraging innovation, self-reliance, and sustainable development. When external aid substitutes for internal growth, nations may become ensnared in cycles of dependency, where progress stagnates, resilience erodes, and self-pride diminishes. True empowerment comes not from perpetual assistance but from creating opportunities for self-sufficiency, education, and economic growth.

Understanding these ripple effects is crucial for ensuring that generosity serves as a positive force. By recognizing the potential negative consequences of unbalanced generosity, we can promote growth, empowerment, and authentic connections rather than unintentionally fostering dependency or cycles of emotional strain.

THE BURDEN OF UNHEALED WOUNDS: WHEN GENEROSITY TURNS PAINFUL

Generosity, often seen as a hallmark of kindness and empathy, can take a dark turn when it is driven by unresolved trauma or emotional wounds. While giving is frequently celebrated as a virtuous act, the motivations behind unchecked generosity can stem from a place of pain rather than abundance. When this occurs, generosity can transform into a burden—one that leads to self-sacrifice, resentment, and emotional exhaustion. This chapter delves into the complex relationship between unhealed wounds and acts of giving, exploring the hidden costs of unchecked generosity.

PATHOLOGICAL ALTRUISM: THE ROOTS OF UNCHECKED GENEROSITY

For some individuals, the urge to give stems from past experiences of trauma, neglect, or emotional pain. In these cases, generosity is not primarily about meeting the needs of others. Instead, it becomes a coping mechanism aimed at seeking validation, repairing self-worth, or avoiding the confrontation of unresolved emotions. This form of giving fills an emotional void within the giver rather than genuinely addressing the recipient's needs.

Unchecked generosity, often fueled by unresolved trauma, creates a rich emotional landscape for the giver. It involves a complex interplay of emotions: the satisfaction of helping others, the fear of rejection or inadequacy, and the frustration of feeling unappreciated or taken for granted. This emotional complexity can obscure the toll such generosity takes on the giver's well-being.

While they may rationalize their actions as selfless or noble, they simultaneously grapple with resentment, exhaustion, or dissatisfaction.

This dynamic is closely tied to pathological altruism, a condition where excessive or compulsive giving arises not from a genuine desire to help but from unresolved emotional issues. Although such behavior may appear virtuous on the surface, it's important to recognize that pathological altruism can ultimately harm both the giver and the recipient.

For instance, someone who grew up in an environment where love and affection were conditional may learn to associate giving with acceptance or approval. In this case, excessive giving becomes a way to seek the validation they lacked as a child. Similarly, individuals who have experienced rejection or abandonment may use generosity to forge connections or maintain relationships, driven

by the fear that withholding generosity will lead
to further isolation.

Often, these motivations operate
unconsciously, making it difficult for the giver to
recognize that their generosity is not entirely
selfless. Instead, they are influenced by unmet
emotional needs that generosity cannot fulfill.
This unconscious influence sheds light on the
hidden complexities of giving, and left
unchecked, this cycle of giving can lead to
emotional and material exhaustion,
resentment, and the inability to establish
healthy boundaries, thereby reinforcing the
very wounds the giver seeks to heal.

THE COST OF SELF-SACRIFICE

When generosity stems from unhealed
wounds, it frequently leads to patterns of self-
sacrifice. The giver prioritizes others' needs
above their own, often to the detriment of their
physical, emotional, or financial well-being.
Over time, this self-sacrificial behavior can

result in burnout, as the giver exhausts their resources without replenishing them.

Self-sacrifice is particularly common among individuals who struggle with feelings of unworthiness or guilt. They may feel that they must constantly prove their value through acts of generosity, believing that their worth is tied to their ability to give. This mindset can trap them in a cycle of over-giving, where they neglect their own needs in favor of meeting others' expectations.

For example, a parent who feels guilt over past mistakes might overcompensate by giving excessively to their children, even at the expense of their own well-being. Similarly, a friend who fears rejection might always be the one to lend money, offer emotional support, or go out of their way to help, even when it causes personal strain.

THE EMERGENCE OF RESENTMENT

Unchecked generosity, particularly when it is not reciprocated or appreciated, often gives rise to resentment. The giver may begin to feel unappreciated, taken advantage of, or trapped in a one-sided relationship. However, they may struggle to express these feelings openly, fearing conflict or rejection.

Resentment can also stem from a mismatch between the giver's expectations and the receiver's response. When generosity is driven by an unconscious desire for validation or recognition, the giver may feel disappointed or hurt if their efforts go unnoticed or unacknowledged. This disappointment can build over time, creating tension within relationships.

For instance, someone who frequently lends emotional support to friends may grow resentful if those friends do not offer the same level of support in return. Similarly, an employee who regularly takes on additional tasks to help colleagues may feel exploited if their efforts are not recognized or rewarded.

EMOTIONAL EXHAUSTION AND COMPASSION FATIGUE

When generosity becomes a coping
mechanism for unhealed wounds, it can lead to
emotional exhaustion and compassion fatigue
in personal relationships. Individuals who
consistently prioritize others' needs over their
own often find themselves emotionally and

physically drained. This kind of exhaustion is widespread among those who provide ongoing support to loved ones, such as parents, partners, or friends, often at the expense of their own well-being.

Compassion fatigue arises when the emotional toll of giving becomes overwhelming, and the giver can no longer maintain the same level of care or empathy. Over time, this can manifest as burnout, emotional detachment, or numbness. For instance, someone who has always been the one to listen, offer advice, or provide support may find it increasingly difficult to continue offering that support when their own emotional needs are ignored. As a result, they may begin to feel unnoticed or unappreciated, leading to frustration, hurt, and, eventually, anger.

This fatigue can significantly damage relationships, particularly when generosity is closely tied to an individual's sense of self-worth or identity. The giver may feel inadequate or like they are failing their loved ones by not being able to maintain their usual level of care. The emotional toll that goes unacknowledged can breed resentment or guilt, leading the giver to question their role in the relationship and sometimes feel isolated. They may feel uncomfortable expressing their fatigue or dissatisfaction out of fear of conflict or rejection.

Compassion fatigue also affects communication and connection within relationships. Overwhelmed and exhausted, the giver may withdraw emotionally, become irritable, or avoid confrontation, fearing that their needs will be dismissed. This emotional withdrawal can lead to misunderstandings, distance, and a breakdown in the relationship, as the other person may not understand the underlying reasons for the giver's behavior.

If left unaddressed, emotional exhaustion and compassion fatigue can significantly disrupt relationship dynamics, leaving both parties feeling unfulfilled and misunderstood. Recognizing the signs of fatigue and setting healthy boundaries is crucial to protect the giver's well-being and preserve the relationship's health.

Unchecked generosity, especially when motivated by unresolved trauma, can also create imbalances within relationships. The giver may unintentionally foster dependency, while the receiver may feel pressured or obligated to reciprocate. This lack of balance can blur boundaries, making it difficult for both individuals to establish clear expectations. The giver may struggle to say no, even when their resources are limited, while the receiver may feel guilty for accepting help or uncertain about how to respond.

Unchecked generosity can sometimes attract individuals who take advantage of the giver's willingness to help, creating cycles of manipulation and dependency that further drain the giver's emotionl and material resources. This deepens their burden, making it even more challenging to maintain healthy relationships and reinforcing patterns of over-giving that stem from unhealed wounds.

The weight of these unresolved emotional wounds highlights the need for greater awareness and reflection. While generosity can be a powerful force for good, it must be balanced with self-awareness, boundaries, and an understanding of one's motivations. Without these safeguards, Giving may become more harmful than beneficial, both for the giver and those around them, if they become entirely dependent on the giver. By recognizing the complexities of unchecked generosity, we can address its hidden toll, fostering healthier and more sustainable patterns of giving that nurture connection and well-being.

THE FIVE KINDS OF PATHOLOGICAL GENEROSITY

Generosity is often celebrated as an unquestioned virtue, a sign of compassion, selflessness, and moral character. Across cultures and throughout history, the act of giving has been revered, encouraged, and woven into the fabric of human relationships. However, generosity is not a singular concept; it takes many forms, each with its complexities, motivations, and potential pitfalls. While giving is often viewed as inherently good, an unexamined or excessive approach to generosity can lead to unintended consequences, including personal burnout, relational imbalances, and even harm to the recipient. It's crucial to be aware of these potential pitfalls to ensure that our generosity is always beneficial.

The key to understanding generosity lies in recognizing its multiple dimensions. While material generosity—the giving of money, goods, or tangible resources—is the most visible form, there are several other significant forms of generosity: emotional generosity, intellectual generosity, social generosity, spiritual generosity, generosity of time and energy, and generosity of Intimacy. Each of these plays a vital role in shaping human interactions, influencing both the giver and receiver profoundly. When taken to excess, however, these forms of giving can lead to harm.

Material generosity is often seen as a direct expression of compassion and empathy, a way to address inequality, and a means of fostering social cohesion. However, the line between virtuous giving and a harmful cycle is delicate. When material generosity becomes excessive, unexamined, or motivated by external pressures, it can shift from a laudable virtue to a pattern that perpetuates harm and imbalance. In some cases, it may inadvertently create a sense of dependency in the recipient, undermining their autonomy and perpetuating a cycle of reliance.

Generosity, in its essence, is meant to uplift individuals and strengthen communities. However, it can also become a source of imbalance and tension when driven by unhealthy motivations or unexamined dynamics. This is particularly evident when generosity stems from ego-driven motives, such as a subconscious need for validation, fear of rejection, or unresolved emotional wounds.

The key difference between healthy and pathological generosity lies in the motive behind the action. Pathological generosity often arises from a deep-seated emotional need, such as seeking approval or attempting to cope with low self-esteem. Excessive giving may serve as a way to gain control, validate self-worth externally, or avoid feelings of inadequacy. This type of generosity can negatively impact both the giver and the recipient.

This chapter explores the intricate interplay of religious, cultural, and societal factors that shape material generosity. It also serves as a guide to the risks and challenges associated with unchecked giving. By understanding the complexities of generosity, we can explore potential solutions and strategies to prevent harm and promote a more balanced, mindful approach to giving.

Material Generosity

Emotional Generosity

Generosity of Time and Energy

Intellectual Generosity

Intimacy and Sexual Generosity

Each form of generosity carries its own set of benefits and challenges. The key to maintaining a healthy approach to giving is self-awareness, understanding the motivations behind our generosity and recognizing when it crosses into self-sacrifice or enables harm. This chapter seeks to explore these seven dimensions, shedding light on both the beauty and the risks inherent in generosity. By cultivating a more balanced approach to giving, we can foster healthier relationships, maintain our well-being, and ensure that our generosity truly serves its intended purpose. With self-awareness, we can navigate the complexities of generosity with confidence and control.

This introduction serves as a foundation for the deeper exploration of each form of generosity in this chapter. By understanding the multifaceted nature of giving, we can navigate its complexities with greater mindfulness, ensuring that our generosity uplifts rather than depletes.

PATHOLOGICAL MATERIAL GENEROSITY

Generosity is often celebrated as a virtue, but there is a darker, more complex side to it—pathological material generosity. This occurs when giving becomes excessive, compulsive, or driven by unresolved psychological wounds or a misunderstanding of the immediate, tangible security in the give-and-take nature of relationships, such as financial support or essential documents. When giving becomes repetitive, it shifts from generosity to a transactional nature. At this point, it should be recognized as a debt or contractual arrangement, but many fail to make this distinction. Unrealistic expectations can arise when individuals misjudge the complexities of human nature, assuming that others will reciprocate as they themselves would, which often leads to disappointment and a loss of time and money. Whether rooted in personal trauma or an idealized view of others, pathological generosity can fuel self-destructive behaviors driven by a deep need for validation, fear of rejection, and insecurity. Some individuals give excessively in an attempt to gain love, approval, or a sense of self-worth. Others use material generosity as a way to avoid emotional intimacy, mistakenly believing that gifts and financial support can replace genuine connection. Over time, this type of giving becomes burdensome for both the giver and the receiver. Despite their good intentions, the giver ends up emotionally depleted, not receiving the same care they freely offer—even when it comes from a place of pain.

Though these individuals are genuinely good people who want to help, they often overlook their own need for reciprocity. They may not fully understand why they feel depressed or unlucky in relationships, yet deep down, their inner selves recognize that they deserve care, appreciation, and reciprocation. They haven't yet connected with this part of themselves, and with their unconscious idealism, they may go through life without examining their own needs. They may struggle to assert their feelings and be "selfish" by putting their own needs first, unaware that acknowledging and embracing their desires for reciprocity is valid and necessary. There is no shame in recognizing the importance of mutual exchange and taking care of one's own emotional well-being.

This imbalance in both types of giving disrupts relationships, ultimately leading to disappointment, resentment, and emotional distress. What starts as an act of kindness or love gradually becomes a burden, leaving both parties unfulfilled. Pathological generosity, though initially well-intentioned, ultimately damages the giver's emotional well-being, creating unhealthy, imbalanced relationships. The toll on the giver's emotional health is significant, underscoring the need for a balanced approach to giving and receiving.

In some cases, generosity is used as a tool for manipulation or control, transforming it into something self-serving. This creates a dynamic where the recipient becomes trapped in a cycle of dependency or obligation, eroding their autonomy and social standing. Unlike healthy generosity, which fosters connection and mutual well-being, this kind of pathological generosity depletes the giver emotionally, breeds resentment, and can even lead to manipulation. It is often more about the giver's need to assert dominance than genuinely addressing the recipient's needs. This can be damaging to the receiver, as they become a source of sustenance for the giver.

In this case, the giver may not be inherently good but rather someone who uses generosity as a means of control. Often, these individuals come from a place of financial stability or a better position than the recipient, so material generosity may not be a significant sacrifice for them. This dynamic is pervasive in certain marital relationships, where one partner uses generosity as a tool to assert power and control over the other.

Examples of Interpersonal Relationships
The Friend Who Buys Affection

Sarah has always been the one to pay for dinner, buy expensive gifts, and lend money without hesitation, believing that her generosity secures her friends' loyalty and appreciation. However, over time, she begins to feel taken advantage of when her friends rarely reciprocate or show the loyalty and respect she expects. She realizes that when people receive things without obligation, they may begin to disrespect the giver, often as a way to mask their own shortcomings or lack of investment in the relationship. Sarah starts to resent her friends, feeling as though they only keep her around for what she can give them. Her friends are taken aback when she finally expresses her frustration, claiming they never asked for extravagant gifts but took everything she offered. Instead of fostering closeness, Sarah's generosity created an imbalance that left her feeling unappreciated and hurt. The relationship eventually ends, and Sarah finds herself isolated. These so-called friends, often lacking moral depth, took advantage of her, denying any responsibility or reciprocation. However, as Sarah heals from her wounds and stops her unconscious generosity, she attracts a new circle of friends—people who are conscious, kind, and moral—who understand the value of mutual respect and reciprocity.

The Parent Who Gives and Feels Unappreciated

Michael's father never says "I love you" or supports him in complex social situations, yet he constantly showers him with gifts and money to make his life easier. While this financial generosity may ease some immediate struggles, it never compensates for the emotional support Michael truly needs. Lacking a genuine connection with his father, he seeks support elsewhere, yet he struggles to stand on his own and build a successful life. Having never faced financial hardship, had to provide for himself, or experienced true scarcity as a child, he has not developed the resilience necessary to navigate the world independently.

When Michael voices his frustrations, his father focuses only on the financial support he has given, believing it should be enough. However, because Michael never had to earn his own way, he struggles to appreciate the value of money. Coupled with the absence of emotional guidance to develop inner strength, this lack of life experience stunts his growth. In response to Michael's complaints, his father retorts, "After everything I've done for you, this is how you repay me—by saying I haven't done anything for you?"

Michael begins to feel trapped, realizing that his father's generosity overlooked what truly mattered—emotional support and the development of resilience. He grows resentful without the tools to navigate life's challenges or the confidence to stand on his own. He feels misunderstood, and their relationship becomes increasingly strained. This dynamic breeds guilt and emotional turmoil, leaving Michael indebted for the financial support while lacking the life skills and emotional foundation he needs to thrive.

The Partner Who Over-Gives

Emily believes love is best expressed through grand gestures, so she spares no expense In showering her partner, Jake, with extravagant gifts, elaborate vacations, and unwavering financial and emotional support. She invests in his dreams, helps him advance in his career, and stands by him through every hardship, believing that her generosity will strengthen their bond and secure their future together.

Jake, however, views success and financial independence differently. As a man, he values being the provider and sees his achievements as central to his identity. While he initially accepts Emily's support, he eventually begins to feel emasculated by her constant giving. Instead of appreciating her sacrifices, he starts to resent them, seeing her generosity as overbearing rather than loving. As his career flourishes—mainly due to Emily's help—he gradually distances himself, no longer feeling the same attachment or sense of obligation toward her.

When he finally leaves to pursue a relationship where he can assert his role as the breadwinner, Emily is devastated—not just emotionally but also financially, having lost years of her life to a one-sided investment. She gave without limits, believing her selflessness would guarantee Jake's loyalty, but instead of receiving gratitude, he abandoned her. She watches the dreams she built around their future shatter, leaving her alone with the painful realization that no one truly valued her generosity.

Her heartbreak deepens as she faces the harsh truth—she had been so consumed by the joy of giving that she ignored the potential consequences. She assumed love meant giving endlessly, without expectation or safeguards, never considering the need for reciprocity or mutual commitment. Yet deep down, her soul longed for recognition, appreciation, and a love that matched hers. Ultimately, she is left to rebuild her life, learning that love must be a balance of give-and-take in real time or secured through an explicit agreement. Love should never be a sacrifice that leaves her depleted and broken.

The Toxic Cycle of Generosity in Sibling Relationships

Toxic generosity within sibling relationships can be especially painful, often stemming from deep childhood wounds and a desperate yearning for love and connection. One sibling, shaped by emotional neglect or a strong need to feel valued—whether due to childhood

neglect or their position in the sibling
hierarchy—may take on the role of the giver.
This sibling offers financial help, emotional
support, and endless sacrifices in hopes of
fostering closeness. While their generosity
comes from a place of good intentions, it often
becomes excessive, driven by an unconscious
desire to heal unmet childhood needs. The
giver believes that their acts of kindness will
bridge the emotional gaps they feel. Still, the
imbalance gradually creates resentment and
emotional exhaustion, both for the giver and
the receiver.

The receiving sibling, meanwhile, may come to
depend on this generosity, sometimes without
recognizing the imbalance it creates. They
might think of their sibling as simply a kind and
selfless person, yet deep down, they know they
would never do the same if the roles were
reversed. Over time, entitlement replaces
gratitude, and they begin to view their sibling's
giving as an obligation rather than an act of

love. When the giver eventually reaches a breaking point and seeks emotional or material reciprocity, the receiving sibling often responds with resentment or even anger. They justify their lack of reciprocity by insisting that the giver always acted out of their own free will, dismissing the emotional toll it took.

This toxic cycle leaves the generous sibling feeling used and unappreciated while the other remains unaware of the harm they've caused. In many cases, this dynamic can ultimately fracture the relationship, as the giver realizes their generosity was never about mutual care but rather about filling a void within themselves that their sibling was all too willing to exploit. True healing requires the giver to set boundaries, recognize their own worth beyond what they provide, and understand that love should be mutual—not a one-sided sacrifice that leaves them emotionally depleted.

Marital Toxic Generosity: A Manipulative Cycle in Relationships

Imagine a man who showers a woman with gifts, emotional support, and financial assistance while courting her. He buys her lavish presents, takes her on extravagant trips, and ensures she never lacks anything. His generosity seems endless, and his intentions appear pure—he wants to prove his love and make her feel valued. She begins to feel secure and cherished, believing that this generosity shows how much he cares.

However, once they are married, the dynamic shifts dramatically. The man, now in a position of control, isolates her from her friends and family, subtly undermining her independence. He still provides financial support, but his generosity is no longer given freely; it becomes conditional. He criticizes her spending habits and limits her access to money, making her feel guilty for any financial decision that doesn't align with his desires. What was once an act of love has now become a manipulation tool.

Whenever she expresses the need for more independence or questions his behavior, he reminds her of everything he's done for her. He gives with one hand but takes away her autonomy with the other. He constantly frames his generosity as a gift she should be grateful for, using it as leverage to control her actions, decisions, and even her sense of self-worth. In his mind, the generosity he once showed is now a form of ownership, making her feel indebted to him, unable to leave or assert her own needs.

Feeling trapped and conflicted, the woman begins questioning whether she truly deserves to make her own choices. Over time, the kindness she once saw as love becomes a suffocating force, and she realizes that the man's generosity was never about partnership or equality but about gaining power and control.

The Illusion of Generosity: When Wealth Masks Abuse

Imagine a wealthy friend who always pays for everything—dinners, vacations, gifts. He claims it's no trouble, and his generosity seems boundless. Yet, despite his outward kindness, he disrespects and bullies his friends, often in the guise of jokes. Despite this, everyone praises his generosity. "He's such a generous person," they say. "He must be a great guy. He has a bit of a temper, that's all."

At first, his friends are grateful for his generosity, enjoying the luxury of his financial support and his outward kindness. But over time, his generosity begins to feel less like kindness and more like a subtle form of control. Whenever someone disagrees with or challenges his actions, he loses his temper, snapping at or belittling them. His outbursts are brief but leave a lingering tension that becomes harder to ignore. Yet his friends brush it off, rationalizing his behavior due to stress or high expectations. After all, he's so generous— surely, he couldn't be a bad person.

The cycle continues: He showers them with gifts and financial assistance, but when his temper flares, he dismisses it with excuses. "I'm just under a lot of pressure," he says, or "I didn't mean it, I was just frustrated." His friends start to internalize these justifications, convincing themselves that his outbursts must not be that bad if he's so generous. Maybe they're overreacting. Perhaps they're too sensitive. Slowly, they begin to downplay the emotional toll his behavior takes on them, telling themselves that their discomfort isn't justified.

As they gaslight themselves, they lose sight of their own needs and boundaries. What once felt like friendship becomes a relationship of dependency—on his generosity, yes, but also on the emotional toll he exacts. They start to feel guilty for being upset, rationalizing that his anger is somehow their fault. They lose self-respect, doubt their instincts, and let their wealth and generosity close their eyes to the toxic pattern developing before their eyes.

This dynamic leaves them emotionally drained, constantly walking on eggshells, afraid to challenge their behavior for fear of triggering another outburst. They've been conditioned to believe that his financial generosity compensates for his emotional volatility, and, over time, they lose their sense of self. What once seemed like a gift becomes a tool of manipulation, keeping them trapped in a cycle where they feel indebted to him for everything—while he continues to abuse their trust and respect.

The Emotional Toll of Over-Giving

Excessive generosity often leads to deep emotional wounds when expectations are unmet. The giver may feel unappreciated, while the receiver may feel burdened or manipulated. Over time, this dynamic can result in feelings of:

Resentment: When the giver feels their efforts are unnoticed or unreciprocated.

Guilt: When the receiver feels obligated to accept gifts or meet unspoken expectations.

Disillusionment: When the giver realizes their generosity has not led to the closeness or appreciation they desired.

Exhaustion: When the giver overextends themselves financially or emotionally, leading to burnout.

Breaking the Cycle of Pathological Generosity

To cultivate healthier relationships, it is crucial to:

Examine Motives: Ask whether generosity stems from genuine kindness or a more profound emotional need for validation or control.

Set Boundaries: Recognize that love and loyalty should not be earned through material means.

Prioritize Emotional Connection: Invest in quality time and emotional intimacy rather than relying solely on material expressions of affection.

Recognize When to Stop: Understand that excessive giving does not always result in stronger relationships, it can sometimes do the opposite.

By shifting from compulsive material generosity to a balanced, mindful approach to giving, relationships can be built on genuine connection rather than unspoken expectations, ensuring both parties feel valued, respected, and emotionally fulfilled.

EMOTIONAL GENEROSITY: NURTURING OR NUMBING

Emotional generosity, a profound expression of care, can manifest as empathy, support, and unwavering presence for others. It's seen in a friend who always listens, a partner who provides steady reassurance, or a family member who offers comfort in times of need.

These are all examples of healthy emotional generosity. However, when given excessively or unconsciously, it can become a double-edged sword—leading to self-neglect, exhaustion, and a gradual erosion of personal identity, often resulting in being taken for granted. This underscores the need for balance and self-awareness in emotional giving.

The distinction between nurturing others and using generosity as a means of emotional numbing is often subtle. For some, constantly attending to others' needs becomes a way to avoid confronting personal struggles. This redirection of emotional energy may offer temporary relief but ultimately serves as a coping mechanism that perpetuates self-neglect and prevents true healing. Over time, the giver may become trapped in a cycle where their sense of self-worth is intertwined with how much they can provide for others, making it

Amy Law

difficult to step back or acknowledge their own
needs.

This cycle is reinforced by societal norms that
often praise selflessness while overlooking its
toll. Acts of emotional generosity may be met
with gratitude and recognition, further
reinforcing the behavior. At the same time, the
fear of rejection or conflict can make setting
boundaries feel risky, leading to a reluctance to
prioritize personal well-being. This underscores
the need for individual self-awareness and
boundary-setting in the face of societal
reinforcement of over-giving.

The Hidden Wounds Beneath Generosity

While emotional generosity is often seen as
selflessness, it can sometimes mask
unresolved personal trauma. Those who give
endlessly may find themselves caught in a
cycle of perpetual empathy, feeling guilty if
they do not fully absorb the pain of others.
What begins as a sincere act of kindness can

evolve into an unconscious coping mechanism—a way to seek the care and validation they struggle to receive.

Ironically, this dynamic can deepen loneliness rather than alleviate it. As people become accustomed to their unwavering support, the giver often finds that the same level of care is not reciprocated. Over time, emotional generosity shifts from a fulfilling exchange to an exhausting obligation, draining the giver while reinforcing their underlying wounds. This imbalance in relationships can take a significant emotional toll, and it's essential to recognize and empathize with the givers who find themselves in this situation.

When the Wounded Ego Seeks Recognition Through Giving

Beyond trauma and self-sacrifice, emotional generosity can also be a way for a wounded ego to seek validation. Those who have experienced emotional neglect, abandonment, or rejection may develop an ego that craves recognition, appreciation, and a sense of importance. When self-worth becomes intertwined with being needed, excessive giving transforms into an unconscious pursuit of significance.

The more they give, the more their ego inflates, creating the illusion of strength, selflessness, and indispensability. They become emotional anchors for others, believing their value lies in their ability to provide unwavering support. But this chase for fulfillment through over-giving is a paradox—the more they give, the emptier they feel. This paradox underscores the need for self-awareness and addressing one's own emotional needs in the face of over-giving as a way to seek validation.

The Cycle of Over-Giving and Emotional Depletion

Because their sense of self-worth is deeply tied to their role as a giver, stepping back or setting boundaries feels like a personal failure and loss of identity. Guilt, shame, and fear arise when they cannot offer the same level of emotional support, as though their value diminishes to themselves if they are not constantly tending to others, which is the biggest fear. Over time, this pattern becomes ingrained, and the expectation of their emotional labor becomes an unspoken obligation rather than a choice.

As people come to rely on their constant generosity, the giver finds it increasingly difficult to voice their own needs or ask for support. They may convince themselves they are strong enough to endure the imbalance, but the weight of unreciprocated care eventually leads to exhaustion, disillusionment, and emotional burnout. This emotional exhaustion is a clear sign of the need for self-care, and it's important for givers to recognize and address their own needs.

Emotional Generosity as a Coping Mechanism

For some, emotional generosity serves as an unconscious coping strategy to divert attention from unresolved trauma. By immersing themselves in others' struggles, they can temporarily avoid confronting their pain, fears, or insecurities. This redirection of emotional energy provides a fleeting sense of validation, yet it often leaves their own emotional needs neglected and unaddressed. Self-awareness plays a crucial role in recognizing these patterns and understanding the need to address one's own emotional needs.

This pattern is pervasive among individuals who have experienced neglect, abandonment, or emotional invalidation. Prioritizing the well-being of others becomes a learned survival mechanism—an attempt to gain acceptance or avoid rejection. While this role may have once offered comfort or security, it becomes unsustainable over time, leading to emotional exhaustion, resentment, and internalized frustration.

The Hidden Cost of Emotional Burnout

When emotional generosity is driven by avoidance or self-sacrifice, it inevitably leads to burnout. This state is marked by overwhelming fatigue, emotional detachment, and a diminishing ability to offer care. Those experiencing burnout may begin withdrawing from relationships, resenting the people they once felt compelled to support, or questioning their capacity to continue giving at the same level.

Burnout manifests in physical exhaustion, irritability, and deep emptiness or disconnection. For those who have built their identity around being a caregiver, it can be particularly devastating, shaking their sense of self-worth and leaving them feeling unfulfilled.

One of the most insidious aspects of emotional burnout is its gradual onset. Many emotional givers dismiss their needs, pushing themselves beyond their limits out of duty or obligation. They continue to give despite their exhaustion—until they reach a breaking point where they can no longer sustain the very role they once found purpose in.

The Impact on Relationships

Although emotional generosity can strengthen relationships, it can also create imbalances that strain these connections over time. When one person consistently assumes the emotional support and morale-giver role, it can foster dependency in the receiver and expectancy. In contrast, the giver may feel neglected or unappreciated. This imbalance can erode trust, mutual respect, and the overall quality of the relationship. We must be cautious of these dynamics and strive for a balanced exchange of emotional support in our relationships.

Receivers may unintentionally rely on the giver's emotional support, assuming that the giver's capacity is limitless. They may fail to recognize that the giver's emotional resources are finite. Conversely, the giver may feel taken for granted, leading to resentment and frustration, which strains their bond.

This dynamic is further complicated by societal expectations, particularly for women, who are often expected to take on emotional labor in family, workplace, and community settings. These cultural norms can burden individuals unfairly, leaving them vulnerable to the pitfalls of excessive emotional generosity and burnout. Awareness of these societal influences and their impact on our emotional health is crucial.

Cultural and Societal Influences

Cultural and societal factors play a significant role in shaping attitudes toward emotional generosity. In many cultures, empathizing, nurturing, and providing emotional support are seen as virtues, especially for women and caregivers. These expectations can pressure individuals to overextend emotionally, even at the cost of their well-being.

The Role of Personal Trauma

Unresolved trauma often lies at the heart of unhealthy patterns of emotional generosity. Those who have experienced trauma may develop a heightened sensitivity to the emotions and needs of others. Their own painful experiences teach them the importance of empathy and understanding. However, this sensitivity can also make them more likely to neglect their emotional boundaries, prioritizing others' needs over their own.

Trauma survivors may also struggle with feelings of unworthiness or guilt, driving them to overcompensate through acts of emotional generosity. They may believe their value lies in their ability to care for others, leading them to give excessively to validate their self-worth.

The Emotional Toll of Unhealthy Giving

When emotional generosity morphs into self-sacrifice, it heavily affects the giver's mental and emotional health. Over time, the constant outpouring of emotional energy leaves individuals feeling drained, disconnected, and unfulfilled. They may begin to question their motivations, wondering whether their acts of kindness genuinely benefit others or are merely a means of avoiding their emotional pain.

This chapter reminds us of emotional generosity's complexities and its inherent challenges. While giving is an inherently valuable act, it is vital to recognize the fine line between nurturing others and neglecting oneself. By understanding the factors that drive emotional generosity, and the potential risks associated with unchecked giving, we can foster a more balanced and mindful approach to generosity that considers both the needs of others and our well-being.

Finding True Fulfillment Beyond the Ego's Chase

True emotional generosity should enrich, not deplete. It thrives when given freely, not as a means of validation or self-neglect.

Recognizing when giving is driven by a need for external affirmation, avoidance of personal pain, or fear of rejection is crucial in breaking unhealthy cycles. Learning to set emotional boundaries, practice self-care, and allow oneself to receive as much as giving is essential for cultivating healthy, fulfilling relationships.

Stepping away from overgiving does not mean abandoning compassion means creating space for authentic, mutual connections. When emotional generosity is no longer tied to ego's hunger for validation, it becomes an actual act of love for others and oneself.

Real-Life Examples of Emotional Generosity in Relationships

Emily and Her Best Friend, Rachel

Emily is the friend everyone turns to for advice, emotional support, or simply a listening ear. Rachel, her best friend, often calls her late at night to vent about her problems, relationship struggles, family issues, and work stress. Emily always listens patiently, offering comfort and solutions. However, when Emily tries to share her struggles, Rachel quickly shifts the conversation back to herself. Over time, Emily starts feeling emotionally drained, realizing that her generosity is a one-way street. She hesitates to set boundaries, fearing she might lose the friendship, but she also begins to feel unseen and exhausted.

James and His Wife, Sarah

James takes pride in being a supportive husband to Sarah. Whenever stressed, he drops everything to comfort her, reassures her when she has self-doubts, and ensures her needs are always met. However, when James faces difficulties at work, he suppresses his stress because he believes his role is to be strong for his wife, not to burden her with his problems. Over time, this unspoken expectation weighs heavily on him. He starts feeling emotionally neglected—not because Sarah doesn't care, but because he has trained himself to only give, not receive.

Michael, the "Neighborhood Therapist"

Michael is known in his community as the person everyone can rely on. Neighbors, friends, and even distant acquaintances come to him with their problems—marital conflicts, financial struggles, emotional crises. He listens, advises, and supports them without hesitation. However, Michael rarely shares his burdens with anyone. His role as the "strong one" has become his identity, and he feels guilty if he ever prioritizes himself. Eventually, he starts feeling overwhelmed and disconnected, realizing that while he helps everyone else, no one is truly there for him.

Olivia and Her Younger Sister, Sophie

As the older sister, Olivia has always cared for Sophie—emotionally, financially, and even as a parental figure at times. Whenever Sophie faces a problem, Olivia is the first to offer support, whether comforting her after a breakup or helping her with college expenses. However, as the years go by, Olivia starts to feel resentment. Sophie has become dependent on her emotional generosity, rarely checking in on Olivia's needs. Olivia begins questioning whether giving is truly an act of love or if it has become an obligation she can't escape.

TIME AND ENERGY – THE PERILS OF OVERCOMMITMENT

Generosity, a virtue celebrated across cultures, is a deeply personal and meaningful act that strengthens human connections and supports those in need. It's not just about material giving; many individuals express their generosity by offering their time, energy, and emotional labor. However, this form of giving, while noble, also carries risks that should not be overlooked. When individuals overcommit without establishing clear boundaries, they may feel overwhelmed, emotionally drained, and resentful.

Time and energy, though intangible, are among the most valuable resources a person can offer. Yet, unchecked generosity in these areas can lead to profound exhaustion, emotional strain, and relationship imbalances. For instance, a person who consistently gives more time and energy to their friends than they receive in return may feel a sense of imbalance in the relationship. Many people feel compelled by a sense of duty or a need to prove their worth by constantly attending to the needs of others without realizing that this pattern of giving may gradually deplete them. This chapter delves into the complexities of overcommitment, shedding light on its psychological roots, hidden costs, and impact on personal relationships.

The Allure of Giving Time and Energy

Unlike financial generosity, which is easily measurable, giving time and energy is often viewed as an ultimate expression of care and devotion. Supporting a struggling friend, mentoring a colleague, volunteering for community initiatives, helping someone clean their house or cook for them, or consistently being available for loved ones are hallmarks of selflessness. This giving fosters connection and reinforces one's sense of purpose, making it inherently rewarding.

Yet, the immeasurable nature of time and energy makes it more challenging to regulate, and since the people they do these things for can do them themselves or hire someone, it might make those givers less valued. People then expect them to do those things, and as in life, everyone has a price; when one gives their goods successfully without any reward or reciprocation, they make their goods cheap, even if it is expensive. Unlike money, which has clear limits, people often struggle to determine how much time and emotional labor they can afford to give before it starts harming their well-being. The desire to help, be useful, or feel needed can lead individuals to commit more than they can handle without realizing the toll it takes on their mental, emotional, and even physical health.

Psychological Drivers of Overcommitment

Several psychological factors contribute to the tendency to overcommit, including the need for validation, fear of abandonment, and internalized cultural expectations.

The Need for Validation

For many, self-worth becomes intertwined with their ability to give. They may believe that their value is measured by how much they support others, leading them to take on more than they can manage. This can be particularly true for individuals who grew up in environments where love and approval were conditional on being helpful or self-sacrificing.

For instance, a person raised in a family where they were expected to mediate conflicts or care for younger siblings might carry this habit into adulthood, feeling an obligation to prioritize others' needs over their own. They may struggle to say no, fearing that refusal will make them seem uncaring or selfish.

Fear of Abandonment

The fear of losing relationships often drives individuals to overcommit and give more than they can sustain. Many worry they will be perceived as disposable or unworthy of meaningful connections if they do not provide enough. This anxiety can trap them in a cycle of overextension, where maintaining bonds comes at a significant personal cost.

Take, for example, an employee who consistently shoulders extra work to support colleagues. They may believe their value in the workplace hinges on their willingness to exceed expectations, fearing that setting boundaries could diminish their worth. Similarly, in personal relationships, someone always available for friends might do so not out of pure generosity but from an underlying fear that saying "no" could result in distance or rejection.

Recognizing and confronting these fears is essential for fostering healthier connections built on mutual respect rather than a constant need to prove one's worth.

Cultural and Social Expectations

Cultural values heavily influence attitudes toward generosity, often defining how people view giving and personal sacrifice. In collectivist societies, self-sacrifice is frequently glorified, symbolizing loyalty, love, and moral strength. This cultural norm can make it challenging for individuals to establish or maintain healthy boundaries, as prioritizing personal needs may be stigmatized as selfish or socially unacceptable.

Religious and moral teachings further reinforce these dynamics. Many belief systems equate selflessness with moral righteousness, framing sacrifice as a pathway to spiritual rewards, such as divine favor or entry into paradise. These teachings often promote unrestrained giving, even when it compromises the giver's well-being or benefits individuals undeserving of the effort. The portrayal of self-sacrifice as a noble ideal fosters societal pressure to prioritize others endlessly, perpetuating an environment where overcommitment is both normalized and praised.

This pressure is particularly evident in the rigid gender roles found across many cultures. Women are often burdened with caregiving responsibilities as mothers, daughters, or partners despite societal claims of gender equality. These expectations are rarely explicitly stated but are deeply embedded in cultural norms, subtly dictating that women must overextend themselves for the benefit of family and community.

Consider, for instance, the woman who sacrifices career advancements to care for aging parents while her male siblings remain uninvolved. Or the wife who juggles household responsibilities without adequate support from her husband, even when both work full-time outside the home. In many families, it is still assumed that the woman will shoulder the additional labor of maintaining a household—emotional, physical, and logistical. These patterns of overcommitment often go unchallenged because they are ingrained in societal definitions of love, duty, and virtue.

Recognizing these cultural and social pressures is crucial for fostering healthier perspectives on generosity. By understanding that giving has limits, individuals can learn to navigate the fine line between healthy generosity and harmful self-sacrifice. This awareness empowers people to honor their boundaries while still making meaningful contributions to those around them, leading to more balanced and fulfilling relationships.

The Hidden Costs of Overcommitment

The consequences of unchecked generosity often go unnoticed until they reach a breaking point. The following are some of the most common effects of overcommitment:

Burnout and Emotional Exhaustion

Burnout occurs when prolonged overcommitment leads to profound physical, emotional, and mental exhaustion, making it difficult for individuals to function effectively in their daily lives. Unlike temporary stress, which typically subsides with rest or resolution, burnout is a chronic state that profoundly impacts one's well-being and interpersonal relationships. It may manifest as persistent fatigue, irritability, a loss of motivation, and a diminished capacity for empathy and emotional engagement.

When individuals reach a breaking point, they may undergo a sudden shift—what can feel like a 180-degree transformation—as they break free from their unsustainable roles. Ironically, those around them often misunderstand such shifts, leading to unfair labels like "crazy."

Initially, those experiencing burnout often push through exhaustion, driven by guilt or a sense of obligation. Over time, however, they begin to withdraw from the relationships they once nurtured, unable to continue giving at the same intensity. This withdrawal can strain connections and leave them isolated—a stark contrast to their earlier sense of purpose and fulfillment.

Consider a parent who consistently prioritizes their children's needs over their health and well-being. Despite their best intentions, the relentless demands may lead to overwhelming fatigue, irritability, and emotional distance, ultimately impairing their ability to parent effectively. What begins as an act of love and devotion may, ironically, diminish the quality of care they provide.

This pattern often extends beyond a single generation. Children observing a parent who perpetually sacrifices their needs may internalize the belief that self-sacrifice is a necessary virtue. They may grow up prioritizing others at the expense of their own goals, repeating the same cycle in their adult lives. This creates a generational legacy where self-sacrifice becomes ingrained as a family value despite its misalignment with sustainable success and personal fulfillment.

Self-sacrifice rarely aligns with long-term success. Whether in parenting, relationships, or professional endeavors, true success often requires setting healthy boundaries, preserving energy, and recognizing that meeting one's needs is essential—not selfish. Breaking the generational curse of self-sacrifice involves teaching future generations that self-care is vital to caring for others.

By acknowledging the risks of burnout and cultivating a balanced approach to generosity, individuals can maintain their well-being, foster meaningful relationships, and model healthier behaviors for those who follow. True success lies not in endless sacrifice but in the wisdom to balance giving with self-care.

Resentment and Relationship Strain

Over time, excessive giving without reciprocation can breed resentment. A person who constantly prioritizes others may feel unappreciated or taken for granted. However, they may struggle to express these feelings openly, fearing conflict or rejection.

Take, for example, a friend who always provides emotional support but rarely receives it in return. They may begin to feel their efforts are one-sided, yet hesitate to voice their frustration, believing it would make them appear selfish.

Loss of Personal Identity

When individuals define themselves primarily through their role as caregivers, supporters, or helpers, they risk losing sight of their needs, aspirations, and identity. This can result in feelings of emptiness, lack of fulfillment, and difficulty recognizing their own desires outside of their obligations to others.

For example, a stay-at-home parent who dedicates all their time to their family may one day struggle with their sense of purpose once their children become independent. Likewise, a dedicated community leader who spends years advocating for others may experience an identity crisis if they ever need to step away.

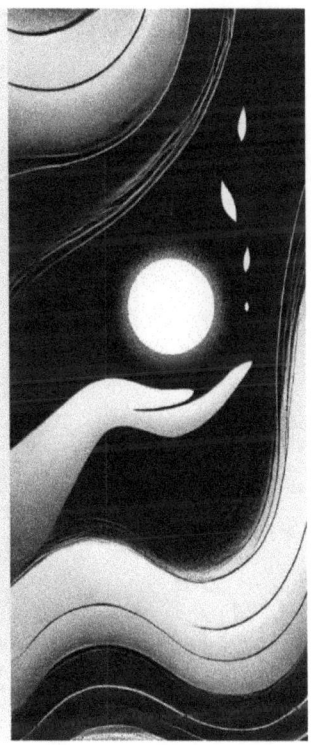

PATHOLOGICAL INTELLECTUAL GENEROSITY

Intellectual generosity involves sharing knowledge, insights, or ideas with others, and in its healthiest form, it fosters open dialogue, growth, and collaboration. However, when driven by ego, this generosity can take on unhealthy characteristics. Rather than serving as a tool for mutual benefit, it becomes a means of inflating one's sense of importance, seeking validation, or dominating conversations. What should be a shared intellectual exchange often turns into a one-sided performance aimed at boosting the giver's self-esteem, frequently at the expense of others.

When intellectual generosity is motivated by the desire to fill a void or feed the ego, it creates an imbalance where the giver's needs overshadow the actual needs of others. This leads to a cycle where validation, praise, and admiration are sought, often undermining genuine, collaborative, and meaningful exchanges. Recognizing this pattern allows for a clearer distinction between truly helpful intellectual contributions and ego-driven performances, which may leave others feeling unheard, belittled, or undervalued.

Constantly Correcting Others

This behavior typically occurs when someone feels the need to assert their intellectual superiority over others. They might interrupt conversations, correcting even small details, not because the correction is necessary, but because it gives them a sense of power or control.

Example: Imagine you're discussing a historical event with friends, and someone constantly interrupts, correcting minor facts, such as dates or names, even though the overall point you're making isn't wrong. They may seem overly focused on "being right" rather than on fostering a collaborative conversation. This behavior often makes others feel uncomfortable or belittled, especially if the corrections seem unnecessary.

Offering Unsolicited Advice

The individual may feel the need to share their knowledge or perspective in every situation, even when it isn't requested or needed. This can stem from a desire to show that they are the "go-to" source for answers or solutions.

Example: At a family gathering, someone might overhear a conversation about someone's new career path and immediately chime in with advice—sometimes overly detailed or technical advice—on how the person should proceed, despite not being asked. They might believe that offering such advice demonstrates their expertise and makes them look more knowledgeable, but it often feels patronizing or presumptive to others.

Dominating Conversations

Instead of having a balanced exchange of ideas, a person driven by intellectual ego may monopolize the discussion, steering it back to topics they are comfortable with or "experts" in.

They often speak in a way that positions themselves as the authority, overshadowing others' voices.

Example: During a work meeting, someone might start discussing a project, and instead of contributing to the collaborative effort, the individual quickly takes over, explaining every technical detail as though no one else could possibly understand or contribute. They might use complex jargon or speak at length, positioning themselves as the only one with the "correct" knowledge.

Over-Explaining or Over-Teaching

This often involves the person giving more information than necessary, elaborating on every little detail to ensure that others understand just how much they know. The underlying goal is to impress others with their expertise.

Example: If someone shares an idea about a new project, the person with ego-driven intellectual generosity might give an extensive lecture on the topic—offering detailed backstory, unrelated facts, or history—just to show that they are the most informed person in the room. While this may sometimes be helpful, it can feel condescending if the explanation is excessive and not aligned with the audience's actual need for information.

Seeking Recognition or Validation for Knowledge

People with this tendency may go out of their way to make sure others recognize their intellectual contributions. They may subtly remind others of their expertise or accomplishments, either during the conversation or after it has ended.

Example: In a casual conversation, someone might mention a book they recently read, and the person with intellectual ego might interrupt to say, "Oh, I've read that book too—actually, I've read everything the author's written, and here's a detailed analysis on it that I wrote myself." This type of statement is less about contributing to the discussion and more about showcasing their intellectual capabilities.

The Ego-Driven Motive:

Validation from Others

The primary ego-driven motive is that the person craves external validation for their intellect. They may feel incomplete or insecure without confirmation that others see them as knowledgeable or smart. In these moments, their worth is tightly connected to how much others admire their intellectual abilities.

Example: After offering unsolicited advice or dominating a conversation, the individual may wait for praise or acknowledgment from others. They might look for verbal affirmations like "You're so smart!" or "I never thought of it that way!" When they don't receive this kind of recognition, they may feel rejected or undervalued, which can drive them to engage in even more dominating behavior next time.

Positioning as a "Guru" or "Expert"

Intellectual generosity, driven by ego, often seeks to establish the individual as the authority or "guru" in a particular area. They may present themselves as the only person who truly understands a subject, positioning others as less knowledgeable or even inferior.

Example: In a professional setting, someone may continually offer insights or "solutions" to problems, acting as though they hold the ultimate knowledge. They might subtly position others in the room as "novices" by making overly technical or complicated statements, even if simpler solutions exist. The result is that they build a reputation as an intellectual leader, but only by making others feel smaller.

Feeding the Ego Through Praise

The act of offering excessive intellectual generosity may ultimately be a strategy to inflate their self-esteem. When others praise their knowledge or wisdom, it reinforces their belief that they are worthy of admiration, and in turn, this praise fuels their ego.

Example: Someone who has repeatedly corrected or over-explained in a group might find themselves waiting for praise after the conversation shifts. They might say things like, "I hope that was helpful, I've studied this topic for years," in hopes that others will acknowledge their expertise or intelligence.

The Impact on Others:

Feeling Overwhelmed or Undervalued: The person on the receiving end may feel drained or belittled by constant corrections or unsolicited advice. What could have been a collaborative exchange of ideas turns into a one-sided lecture or performance.

Social Strain: Over time, others may begin to avoid conversations with the person, knowing that they will be overpowered or that they'll have to endure a barrage of unnecessary intellectual commentary. This can lead to isolation or social friction.

Decreased Trust: When intellectual generosity becomes a means of feeding one's ego, it can lead to a breakdown in trust. People may begin to see the person as self-serving rather than genuinely helpful, and the attempts to showcase knowledge may feel more like a power play than a meaningful contribution.

.

PATHOLOGICAL SEXUAL GENEROSITY AND THE LOSS OF AUTONOMY

In a society that often places a high premium on physical appearance, women are frequently under pressure to seek validation primarily through the eyes of others, particularly men. This societal norm, which we all contribute to in some way, can lead to a woman's self-worth becoming tied to external admiration, making the need to be desired all-consuming. In this relentless pursuit of feeling beautiful and wanted, she may compromise her autonomy, offering herself in ways she believes will secure approval. However, these acts ultimately diminish her dignity and social standing, as she begins to use her body as a form of currency, hoping it will validate her existence.

This behavior can be understood as 'pathological sexual generosity '—a pattern where a woman offers herself from a place of a desperate attempt to heal a deep-seated emotional wound. In simpler terms, it's a situation where a woman feels compelled to give herself sexually, not out of genuine desire, but as a way to fill an emotional void. Often, this wound stems from childhood experiences of being neglected, called unattractive, or labeled as the 'ugly one' within the family. The inner child's bruised ego drives an obsessive quest for validation, a compulsion to prove external beauty and worth at any cost.

In such cases, the woman may become consumed by shallow pursuits, prioritizing physical appearance over other aspects of her identity. This desperation can lead her to seek validation indiscriminately, hoping for external proof that she is desirable. The fear of being unseen or deemed unattractive becomes a powerful force, often overriding her ability to establish healthy boundaries. Each time she offers her body; it is for the false hope of being cherished solely for her looks. Tragically, this behavior invites manipulation, as men who recognize her vulnerability will exploit it.

Her fear of rejection becomes more potent than her desire to maintain autonomy, creating a dangerous power imbalance. This willingness to overextend herself in pursuit of validation only leads to further exploitation. Over time, her sense of self is eroded, and the line between love, control, and shame becomes increasingly blurred.

Young people coming of age can also face this issue. As they are new to social and romantic dynamics, much like newcomers to any market, they may be particularly vulnerable to seeking validation through external approval. Their inexperience often makes them targets for exploitation and manipulation, further compounding their struggle to establish a strong sense of self. This issue is especially prevalent in the entertainment industry, where young individuals are often pressured to be generous with their bodies under the false promise of success. However, more often than not, these promises remain unfulfilled, and the promised success never materializes.

It is essential to distinguish this form of self-destructive behavior from women who engage in sex work as a pragmatic choice—whether due to financial necessity, lack of education, or limited job opportunities. These women may view their work as a practical means of survival rather than a manifestation of inner emotional turmoil. Their motivations often differ significantly from those driven by a desperate need to prove desirability. The key difference lies in the motivation: while both may involve sexual acts, 'pathological sexual generosity' is driven by a need for external validation, while sex work is often a rational economic decision.

Ultimately, no external generosity can heal the profound sense of inadequacy that stems from unresolved childhood pain. The journey to reclaim autonomy and self-worth begins with the understanding that true validation comes from within. Recognizing and addressing these wounds is not just important but essential for breaking free from the cycle of exploitation and reclaiming dignity and agency.

Generosity and Intimacy

In marriage, generosity is often seen as a cornerstone that fosters love and strengthens connection. When rooted in mutual respect and genuine affection, it becomes a meaningful expression of the deep and profound bond between partners. This mutual respect is not just a nice-to-have but a fundamental aspect of healthy relationships that we should all strive for.

In many cultures, marriage is often framed within traditional roles where women are expected to be sexually available to their husbands. These cultural and religious expectations can significantly shape the dynamic of generosity within the marital relationship. In these contexts, sexual generosity is not always a mutual expression of desire and affection; instead, it can be perceived as a duty—an obligation that a wife must fulfill regardless of her own feelings or needs. Religious and cultural teachings frequently reinforce this notion, positioning a woman's failure to meet her husband's sexual expectations as sinful or morally deficient. This framing distorts the nature of marital intimacy, reducing it from a shared connection experience to a burdensome chore.

Such pressures can profoundly impact a woman's sense of autonomy within the marriage. When her worth is tied solely to her ability to satisfy her partner's desires, regardless of how he treats her, the dynamic shifts from one of mutual respect to one rooted in fear, guilt, or obligation. Over time, intimacy may become a transactional act rather than a heartfelt exchange, leading to a gradual erosion of genuine connection and personal fulfillments

The Perils of Digital Validation

The rise of social media and digital communication has complicated the perception and practice of generosity. Online platforms amplify societal pressures, creating environments where individuals feel compelled to display their value and desirability through curated posts, public declarations, or extravagant gestures. The line between genuine connection and exploitation often becomes blurred, leading to unintended consequences.

Some men exploit this desire for admiration, initiating private conversations filled with compliments and attention. These interactions can become addictive, creating a psychological dependency on praise. When these men suddenly withdraw and reappear, they heighten the woman's vulnerability, pushing her to share increasingly private images. This is often the turning point: the man either disappears entirely, leaving the woman devastated by a withdrawal akin to addiction, or escalates the situation by using the images to manipulate, extort, or blackmail her for more intimacy or money.

What begins as a seemingly harmless quest for admiration can spiral into a dangerous loss of power and autonomy. The emotional toll is profound—anxiety, shame, and fear of exposure often lead to social withdrawal and long-term psychological distress. Many women find themselves isolated, with their personal and professional lives damaged by the misuse of private content.

This dynamic highlights a concerning societal pattern where women's worth is often disproportionately tied to their appearance and desirability. The digital landscape amplifies this pressure, encouraging the belief that women must constantly prove their value through visual displays. While showcasing beauty can be empowering when done from a place of confidence—such as leveraging it to build a business or brand, particularly in industries like fashion—it becomes problematic when driven solely by the need for external validation.

Breaking free from this harmful cycle requires a shift in both individual and cultural mindsets. Fostering awareness about digital boundaries and the potential risks involved is crucial. Women should be empowered to protect their content and define their limits without judgment or blame. At the same time, society must move toward valuing individuals for their authenticity, intellect, and meaningful contributions rather than promoting a culture of performative beauty and affection.

It must be noted that not all sharing of images is a form of toxic bodily generosity. When done with dignity and respect, showcasing one's beauty can serve a meaningful purpose, such as leveraging one's appearance to build a business in the beauty or fashion industry. However, it's essential to maintain dignity— undignified images, though seemingly harmless at first, can slowly erode a woman's professional reputation and hinder her success as her business grows.

By cultivating respect and accountability in digital spaces, a safer and more dignified environment can emerge, allowing both women and men to express themselves without falling prey to exploitation or the loss of reputation. Both women and men must challenge societal narratives that reduce individuals to objects of desire. Many women, driven by insecurities, seek attention and validation on social media, often putting themselves at risk, and some young men can also fall prey to these dynamics. The desire for validation leads them into these situations. By shifting these narratives, social media can become a space of equality and mutual respect, fostering healthier interactions and protecting individuals from harm and reputation loss.

THE LAWS OF RECIPROCITY

Psychological Need for Reciprocity

Humans are inherently wired to expect reciprocity in relationships, a fundamental aspect of maintaining trust, respect, and social connection. When one gives, there is an unspoken, subconscious expectation that something in return will follow—tangible or emotional.

The Impact of Emotional Imbalance and Unmet Needs

The fear of alienation often prevents individuals from setting boundaries. However, it's crucial to understand that setting boundaries is not about rejection but self-respect and maintaining emotional balance. Many hesitate to decline requests or assert personal limits, fearing rejection or exclusion from meaningful relationships. This apprehension frequently stems from a deep-seated need for acceptance within family and close friendships. Yet, establishing clear expectations and assessing reciprocity is crucial for maintaining emotional balance and fostering healthier connections.

Close relationships shape an individual's self-perception and interactions with others. Emotional dependence and vulnerability within these bonds often heighten expectations, making harm inflicted by loved ones more impactful than similar actions from acquaintances.

This dynamic can become even more complex for those who grew up without adequate emotional support. The yearning for love, validation, or acceptance that was missing during formative years often manifests as a compulsive need to give—an unconscious attempt to "earn" affection or approval. Ironically, these individuals are usually seen as selfless and giving because they expect nothing in return, reinforcing the cycle of imbalance.

Understanding these patterns and setting mindful boundaries can help individuals protect their emotional well-being while fostering healthier, more reciprocal relationships. With self-awareness, it's possible to recognize these patterns and make conscious choices that restore balance and harmony in our relationships.

Attachment Theory, a key concept in developmental psychology, provides a key explanation for this dynamic. It suggests that early emotional bonds, especially with primary caregivers, are fundamental to development. The resulting emotional wounds can be profound when these bonds are disrupted or betrayed. A breach of trust by a family member or a close friend undermines the security such relationships are meant to provide, often leaving deep psychological scars.

Transference Dynamics, a key concept in psychoanalysis, provides a key explanation for the intensity of emotional pain in close relationships. It refers to the unconscious redirection of feelings from one person to another. Early emotional bonds, especially with primary caregivers, are fundamental to development. The resulting emotional wounds can be profound when these bonds are disrupted or betrayed. A breach of trust by a family member or close friend undermines the security these relationships are meant to provide, often leaving deep psychological scars.

Transference plays a significant role in this dynamic. Unmet emotional needs from childhood often carry over into adult relationships, shaping patterns of excessive giving. Those who lacked adequate support in their formative years may overextend themselves in an effort to receive the love and validation they once yearned for.

Overgiving individuals believe that by giving more—emotionally, materially, or otherwise—they will finally receive the care they crave. They may also gravitate toward emotionally unavailable individuals who resemble figures from their past, reinforcing a cycle of unreciprocated effort.

Unspoken Expectations exacerbate this issue. In close relationships, individuals often assume their needs will be intuitively understood and met. When these expectations go unfulfilled, disappointment and resentment can set in. The principle of *familiarity breeds contempt* and further explains why prolonged closeness can lead to a diminished appreciation of efforts, resulting in loved ones taking each other for granted.

Cognitive Dissonance, a psychological term, also plays a role. It refers to the mental discomfort experienced when holding two or more contradictory beliefs, values, or attitudes. A person may struggle with conflicting beliefs—desiring to see their loved ones as supportive while also recognizing harmful behaviors. This internal tension often leads to confusion, self-blame, or denial, making it difficult to acknowledge and address the emotional harm until it becomes overwhelming.

Ultimately, the deep emotional investment in close relationships makes any imbalance in give-and-take especially painful.

The Trap of Overcompensation

In an attempt to rewrite their past, these individuals often fall into the trap of overcompensation. They become emotional "caretakers" for others, sacrificing their well-being. They give excessively, without boundaries, driven by the fear that stopping will lead to rejection or alienation. Additionally, they strive to be indispensable, hoping that by doing so, they can secure the loyalty or love they never received.

The Obsession to Be the "Kind One"

For some, the need for reciprocity evolves into an obsession with being seen as the "kind one"—the one who always gives, never says no, and sacrifices endlessly for others. This behavior often stems from unresolved childhood wounds, where emotional needs were unmet. These individuals believe that by over giving, they can earn the love and validation they lacked growing up.

The fear of alienation drives them to give excessively, hoping their kindness will be reciprocated affectionately. However, the cycle of over-giving often leads to emotional depletion, as their generosity is not truly valued. They neglect their needs and boundaries, defining themselves by how much they give rather than who they are.

This obsession with being the "kind one" creates an emotional imbalance, where the giver becomes trapped in a role that drains them. They feel invisible and unappreciated, yet continue to give, hoping for validation that never truly comes. Breaking free from this cycle requires self-awareness and setting boundaries so they can find balance and reclaim their emotional well-being.

The Psychological Dynamics of Unreciprocated Giving

Subconscious Perception of the Giver

When one consistently gives without receiving anything in return, the recipient may subconsciously perceive the giver as "less valuable" or "less important." Unreciprocated giving disrupts the perceived balance of power in the relationship, sending a subtle message that the giver does not deserve equal respect or consideration.

Initially, the recipient may appreciate the giver's generosity. However, giving without expectation can shift from being seen as a noble effort to something taken for granted over time. The giver's continued contributions may be dismissed as routine or obligatory, diminishing respect and appreciation.

The Consequences of Imbalanced Giving in Relationships

The Trap of Unreciprocated Giving

The recipient of persistent, unreciprocated giving may develop an unconscious sense of entitlement or superiority. When given the opportunity, human nature often drives individuals to seek control and dominance in relationships. When someone consistently receives without offering anything in return, they may begin to see themselves as superior to the giver.

This sense of entitlement erodes their understanding of the emotional, physical, or financial costs the giver endures. The recipient may come to expect more without recognizing the need for mutual effort, creating an unhealthy dynamic in which the giver is reduced to a mere resource rather than a respected partner in the relationship.

Psychological Impact on the Giver

On the other hand, the giver often begins their journey of generosity with positive intentions—wanting to express care, affection, or support. However, their over-giving is usually a response to unresolved emotional pain. Rather than confronting their own wounds directly, they channel their pain into excessive generosity, hoping to find healing through the act of giving. In doing so, they create a dynamic where someone else benefits from their pain, making reciprocity not just desirable but a rightful expectation.

When their efforts go unacknowledged or unreciprocated, frustration, resentment, and burnout begin to surface. Over time, they may feel emotionally drained and exploited, questioning both their self-worth and the true motives behind their giving. This internal conflict deepens their exhaustion, leaving them vulnerable to feelings of manipulation and disillusionment.

Furthermore, when they attempt to express their own needs, the recipient may dismiss them as "needy" or overly sensitive, further amplifying their pain. This reaction can evoke memories of past rejection or neglect, reinforcing their psychological distress and making it even harder to break free from the cycle of over-giving.

The Impact of Subtle Manipulation and Imbalance

In some relationships, recipients engage in subtle manipulation, either consciously or unconsciously, by continually taking without offering anything in return. Recognizing the giver's compulsion to provide, they exploit this tendency.

This dynamic often appears in family settings or friendships where one person assumes the role of caretaker without acknowledgment. Over time, the giver's self-respect deteriorates, fostering feelings of frustration and powerlessness. They may feel unable to assert boundaries, while the recipient loses respect for them, viewing the giver as incapable of standing up for themselves.

Respect is often given to those who honor themselves by establishing boundaries and sharing from a place of strength. However, givers who struggle to receive often reinforce the imbalance, as they may feel undeserving, or fear being perceived as selfish.

The Role of Expectation vs. Entitlement

Even when a giver claims to expect nothing in return, hidden expectations often linger. These unspoken desires include gratitude, emotional connection, or validation. The giver may feel hurt, frustrated, or disrespected when these expectations are unmet.

Conversely, recipients in such relationships may develop a subconscious sense of entitlement, believing the giver's generosity is automatic and requiring no acknowledgment. This entitlement further reinforces the imbalance, leading recipients to see the giver as a tool for fulfilling their needs rather than an equal partner in the relationship.

The Pressure of Perfectionism

Perfectionism often plays a role in compulsive giving. Givers may feel obligated to always provide, driven by an internal narrative of "I must always help" or "I need to be the perfect partner, parent, or friend."

This relentless pursuit of approval and validation can lead to emotional burnout when efforts go unnoticed or unappreciated. Perfectionism also makes it difficult to set boundaries, as givers feel they are failing when they cannot meet every demand. The result is dissatisfaction, resentment, and further feelings of disrespect

The Devaluation of Giving

Whether material or emotional, giving requires effort. However, recipients often take emotional support, care, and attention for granted. Over time, they may perceive the giver's emotional investment as an unlimited resource to tap into without reciprocation.

This devaluation erodes respect for the giver and diminishes their sense of worth. The more the giver invests emotionally without receiving care or validation, the less they are appreciated, further contributing to emotional exhaustion.

The Exhaustion of Overgiving

Giving without reciprocity can manifest in various forms of exhaustion, including mental fatigue, emotional burnout, and physical symptoms such as headaches or insomnia. The giver often feels like they are carrying an emotional burden alone, creating frustration and resentment.

This imbalance resembles running a marathon without a finish line—the giver continues to pour energy into the relationship without seeing a return. The recipient may remain oblivious to the giver's emotional weight, exacerbating the cycle of disrespect and imbalance.

The Concept of "Toxic Altruism"

Toxic altruism occurs when giving becomes excessive to the point of self-harm. Givers in this dynamic may believe that "giving is always good" while ignoring their needs or well-being. They often struggle to say "no," fearing rejection or alienation.

This unsustainable behavior leads to burnout and resentment. Meanwhile, recipients accustomed to unreciprocated generosity may grow entitled and less appreciative. Over time, the giver loses respect for both himself and the recipient, further damaging the relationship.

The Role of Respect and Validation

Healthy relationships thrive on more than material exchanges—they depend on respect, recognition, and emotional validation.

Reciprocity, where both parties acknowledge and appreciate each other's contributions, reinforces mutual respect. Without validation, the giver may feel "used" rather than valued, undermining the relationship and breeding disillusionment. The absence of respect creates an emotional deficit, leaving the giver feeling inadequate and disrespected.

Power Dynamics and the Breakdown of Relationships

A lack of reciprocity can shift power dynamics within the relationship. The recipient may unconsciously assume dominance, viewing the giver as weak or easily manipulated. This creates an unhealthy imbalance, eroding respect for the giver. As the relationship becomes increasingly unequal, the giver feels devalued, while the recipient continues to expect more, deepening the divide between them.

The Psychological Impact of Disrespect

Whether conscious or unconscious, disrespect leaves lasting psychological scars. For the giver, it leads to frustration, burnout, and resentment. Upon recognizing the imbalance, the recipient may feel guilt, shame, or confusion. Over time, emotional detachment weakens or dissolves the bond entirely. What started as a generous act ended up causing harm, leaving both parties emotionally drained and disconnected.

The Role of Boundaries

Healthy relationships require clear boundaries defining when to give and step back. These boundaries often become blurred or nonexistent in relationships where one person gives without receiving. The giver may continue offering time, energy, or resources—

even at their own expense—driven by fear of rejection or a strong sense of duty.

Without these boundaries, giving becomes compulsive rather than thoughtful. The recipient may begin to view the giver's actions as automatic rather than intentional. This lack of boundaries reinforces disrespect, as the recipient no longer feels a need for gratitude or reciprocation.

The "Self-Worth" Dynamic

Often, giving without expecting anything in return stems from a desire to prove one's worth or demonstrate love. While this may initially feel noble, prolonged patterns of unreciprocated giving can slowly erode the giver's self-esteem.

Giving from a place of insecurity or the need for self-validation often results in feelings of being invisible or undervalued. The giver may start to believe their worth is only tied to what they provide. This dynamic also impacts the recipient, who may subconsciously undervalue the giver, viewing them as someone to be used without consequence.

Falling into the Victim Role

One of the deeper consequences of persistent unreciprocated giving is that the giver may unknowingly fall into a victim mindset. Often, this behavior stems from unresolved childhood pain—emotional wounds that haven't healed. These individuals, carrying the weight of their past, become willing to give excessively to gain validation and love. Unfortunately, others often see the openness to give as a weakness rather than an expression of care.

People tend to notice the giver's willingness to offer without recognizing the emotional scars behind their actions. They often don't look beyond the surface to understand the deeper emotional needs driving the giver. Instead, they exploit this generosity without hesitation because they recognize the giver as someone

who will continue to give. This creates a toxic
dynamic where the giver, who may already feel
emotionally depleted, is seen as a tool or
resource rather than a valued individual.

At the same time, society tends to value what
is hard to come by. When someone is
constantly willing to give, their generosity
becomes undervalued. People naturally
appreciate things they have to work for or put
effort into obtaining. In this way, the giver's
willingness to consistently provide without
boundaries can lead to their lack of genuine
appreciation or respect, reinforcing their sense
of being overlooked or unimportant. Ultimately,
this dynamic leaves the giver trapped in a cycle
of emotional depletion, unable to break free
from the role of the victim of both their past and
present circumstances.

Psychological Fallout

One-sided giving rarely leads to positive
outcomes. The imbalance often breeds

disrespect, resentment, and, eventually, the breakdown of the relationship.

When giving is unreciprocated, it results in emotional exhaustion. The giver becomes drained and bitter, realizing their efforts aren't fostering the emotional connection they crave.

Additionally, recipients may subconsciously perceive the giver as desperate or "needy," which can erode respect over time.

The impact can also be re-traumatizing. When the giver's efforts go unnoticed, are taken for granted, or aren't reciprocated as expected, it triggers memories of past neglect and rejection, reinforcing feelings of unworthiness.

Restoring Balance: The Path to Healthy Relationships

Breaking this toxic cycle requires both parties to develop self-awareness and respect for each other's needs. Givers must learn to set boundaries and give from a place of strength rather than compulsion or insecurity.

Recipients must cultivate gratitude and recognize the value of mutual effort.

Healthy relationships thrive on respect, shared effort, and balanced exchanges. When these elements are present, giving becomes a source of joy rather than a pathway to emotional depletion. The ability to both give and receive creates a foundation for meaningful, lasting connections where both individuals feel valued and empowered.

Breaking the Cycle

To break free from this destructive dynamic, psychological healing often involves:

> **Developing self-awareness:** Recognizing the pattern of transference and understanding its roots.

> **Setting boundaries:** Learning to give without compromising one's well-being or self-respect.

Reparenting techniques: Providing oneself with the emotional support that was missing during childhood.

Therapeutic interventions: Cognitive-behavioral therapy (CBT) and inner-child work can help reframe negative beliefs and foster healthier relationship dynamics.

The Arabic proverb "اتَّقِ شَرَّ مَن أَحْسَنْتَ إِلَيْهِ". (Be careful of the wrath/evil of the one you benefit) captures a psychological phenomenon in which those we help the most, especially close family or friends, can end up hurting us the most. It highlights the paradox that those who receive the most—love, care, or support—can develop resentment, entitlement, or even hostility.

Psychologically, this reflects a fundamental human dynamic: people who benefit from someone's generosity may feel indebted, but over time, negative emotions can surface if the recipient feels entitled or perceives the help as a form of control, and their perspective shifts.

This shift can lead to resentment and disrespect, as assistance that comes too quickly often loses value. Just like money earned through hard work is valued, gifts or help given without effort can be taken for granted and squandered.

This dynamic becomes particularly intense in close relationships. When generosity is consistently given to the receiver freely, the receiver may begin to take the giver for granted or lash out when their expectations are not met. The proverb also serves as a cautionary tale about excessive self-sacrifice. The relationship can become unbalanced if the giver invests too much emotionally, physically, or financially. The recipient may feel burdened or threatened by the giver's expectations, viewing the generosity as manipulative or an assertion of dominance.

Ultimately, the proverb is to be mindful of how generosity and benefits are exchanged in relationships. Healthy boundaries and mutual respect are essential to avoid the giver's psychological harm. The psychology behind giving without reciprocation often leads to disrespect and imbalance, rooted in human nature and the need for reciprocity in relationships. When one person consistently gives without receiving, it triggers feelings of entitlement in the recipient and, ironically, diminishes their respect for the giver.

Building Awareness of the Need for Boundaries

Setting boundaries is essential for maintaining healthy, balanced relationships. Without them, giving can become automatic and expected, diminishing its value. When individuals give with clear intentions and limits, the exchange feels more genuine. The giver and the recipient feel empowered and respected, knowing that generosity is a choice, not an obligation. Boundaries prevent the giver from feeling taken for granted while encouraging the recipient to recognize the true value of what they receive.

The psychology of unreciprocated giving highlights the need for balance and respect. The giver's self-worth erodes without reciprocity, and the recipient's respect may diminish. Healthy relationships thrive on mutual energy exchange, where both parties give and receive in ways that honor each other's time and needs. While giving without expectation is admirable, consistent one-sided giving leads to emotional depletion, imbalance, and a loss of respect.

Establishing short-term, testable relationship goals can help assess whether the other person aligns with one's energy and capacity for reciprocity. This approach ensures that emotional investments are directed toward individuals who value and respect mutual boundaries. One practical strategy for maintaining these boundaries is practicing the 'compassionate no.' For example, when a friend frequently seeks support, a balanced response might be:

"I care deeply about you and want to support you, but I need to protect my own energy right now. Let's find the time when I can be fully present without overextending myself."

This response acknowledges the relationship's importance while maintaining self-respect and reinforcing boundaries. By balancing generosity with self-protection, individuals can cultivate healthier, more sustainable connections free from the fear of alienation.

Prioritizing Self-Care

Generosity is valuable, but self-care is equally important. Taking time for rest, hobbies, and personal growth allows individuals to recharge and give meaningfully. For instance, a caregiver might set aside personal time for enjoyable activities like reading or exercising. Similarly, a professional might establish strict work-life boundaries to ensure time for relaxation and recharge.

Fostering Balance in Relationships

Reciprocity does not require identical returns but should energetically acknowledge the giver's efforts. If a recipient cannot meet the giver's emotional needs, the giver must step back to preserve both their well-being and the relationship itself. Often, withdrawing excessive giving is the most effective way to restore balance.

Open communication about needs and expectations fosters relationships where both parties feel valued and supported. Regularly checking in on the balance of giving and receiving help prevents resentment and the giver's fulfilling connections.

Breaking the Cycle and Cultivating Healthy Relationships: Self-awareness and boundaries are essential to break the cycle of unbalanced giving. Recognizing underlying psychological patterns helps individuals understand when giving becomes harmful. Healthy relationships are built on reciprocity, respect, and validation—elements that signal mutual value, maintain equality, and deepen emotional bonds.

By giving mindfully—setting limits, understanding motivations, and ensuring the well-being of both parties—individuals can foster relationships that thrive on appreciation rather than obligation.

THE ROLE OF CULTURAL, RELIGIOUS, AND SOCIETAL INFLUENCES IN GENEROSITY

Generosity is often framed as a moral and spiritual obligation, shaped by religious teachings, cultural norms, and societal expectations. Many belief systems emphasize selflessness, sacrifice, and charity as pathways to virtue, divine reward, or spiritual fulfillment. While these values promote compassion and collective responsibility, they can also create immense pressure to give—sometimes beyond one's means or at the expense of personal well-being, and this is particularly true for individuals from communities that view generosity as a moral duty, reinforcing the burden of unchecked wounds or unconscious idealism.

Faith-based and culturally tight-knit communities frequently link giving to moral righteousness, salvation, and divine blessings. Some individuals, driven by deep religious conviction, may prioritize generosity over self-care, believing that self-sacrifice is a form of spiritual devotion. However, this can create an imbalance where those who embrace these principles wholeheartedly may find themselves exploited by those who take advantage of their giving nature. This dynamic often results in emotional exhaustion, financial strain, and resentment, as givers continuously sacrifice while recipients benefit without reciprocation.

For instance, in cultures that prioritize familial duty—such as many Asian, African, and Middle Eastern societies—individuals may feel a strong obligation to provide financial support to extended family members, even if it means compromising their own financial security. Similarly, in religious communities such as Christianity, Islam, or Buddhism, charitable acts like tithing, almsgiving, or volunteering may be encouraged as a means to attain spiritual merit. While such practices cultivate solidarity and moral discipline, they can also lead individuals to neglect their needs in pursuing righteousness.

Moreover, these cultural and religious values surrounding generosity can reinforce harmful over-giving patterns, especially for those carrying unhealed emotional wounds. Some individuals may feel compelled to give excessively, equating generosity with worthiness or redemption, even when it is unsustainable. They may attempt to match the level of generosity of those who are more financially secure despite their limitations. In contrast, those without such emotional burdens tend to approach generosity with greater balance. While they still give, they do so in moderation, ensuring that their generosity does not compromise their well-being.

Understanding these influences is crucial in fostering healthier patterns of giving that honor both the virtue of generosity and the necessity of self-preservation. By recognizing the interplay between cultural, religious, and psychological factors, individuals can cultivate a more sustainable and intentional approach to giving, ensuring that their generosity uplifts themselves and those they support.

GENEROSITY IN CHRISTIANITY: PRINCIPLES AND RELIGIOUS LAW

Generosity in Christianity is deeply rooted in the love of God and expressed through various acts of giving, both material and immaterial. It is considered a fundamental virtue, reflecting God's love for humanity and serving as a core expression of a Christian's faith. Christians are called to give willingly, not out of obligation, but from a heart of love and compassion, mirroring the selflessness that Jesus Christ exemplified. In following His example, believers are encouraged to love their neighbors as themselves and God to serve others. Through generosity, Christians help those in need and grow in their faith, becoming more like Christ, who gave everything for humanity's sake. Generosity is not just about giving—it is a way to honor God, deepen one's spiritual journey, and reflect His love to the world.

Amy Law

The Concept of Generosity in Christianity

Generosity in Christianity is understood as an act of Kindness toward others and an expression of gratitude to God for the blessings one has received. The New Testament emphasizes that generosity is a key characteristic of a faithful follower of Christ. Jesus Himself demonstrated generosity by selflessly giving His time, resources, and, ultimately, His life for the salvation of others.

Jesus taught His followers to give without expecting anything in return, to love unconditionally, and to care for society's marginalized, including the poor, the sick, and the oppressed. This principle of self-giving love is central to the Christian understanding of generosity.

In the Gospel of Matthew, Jesus speaks of the importance of giving to others: *"But when you give to the needy, "do not let your left hand know what your right hand is doing so that your giving may be in secret. Then your Father, who sees what is done in secret, will reward you."* (Matthew 6:3-4).

Forms of Gener "city in Christianity

Generosity in Christianity takes various forms, all of which are seen as acts of love and compassion:

Tithing (The Practice of Giving to God)

Tithing refers to giving a tenth of one's income to the church or to the work of God's ministry. The practice is rooted in the Old Testament, where God commanded the Israelites to give a tithe of their produce and livestock as an offering. In the New Testament, while the requirement for tithing is not explicitly emphasized, the principle of giving remains essential. Christians are encouraged to give generously to support the church and to further the gospel's mission.

In the book of Malachi, God challenges His people to give: *"Bring the whole tithe into the "storehouse, that there may be food in my house. Test me in this," says the Lord Almighty, "and s "e if I will not throw open" the floodgates of heaven and pour out so much blessing that there will not be room enough to store it."* (Malachi 3:10)

Charitable Giving

Beyond tithing, Christians are called to give to those in need—whether the poor, the sick, or those suffering injustice. The Bible frequently encourages helping those who are less fortunate, and Jesus Himself modeled this kind of Generosity.

In the Gospel of Luke, Jesus tells His followers to give freely: *"Give to everyone who asks you, "and if anyone takes what belongs to you, do not demand it back."* (Luke 6:30).

Hospitality

Genero "city in Christianity also extends to hospitality. Christians are encouraged to open their homes and hearts to others, especially strangers, the poor, and those in need. The Bible contains many passages that speak to the importance of welcoming others into one's home to show one's Kindness.

In the book of Hebrews, Christians are urged to be hospitable: *"Do not forget to show hospitality" y to strangers, for by so doing some people have shown hospitality to angels without knowing it."* (Hebrews 13:2)

Voluntary Acts "of Kindness

In addition to material gifts, Christians are encouraged to be generous with their time, skills, and abilities. Simple acts of Kindness, such as visiting the sick, comforting the grieving, or volunteering for a good cause, are seen as expressions of Christ-like generosity.

Generosity as a Commandment in Christianity

Generosity in Christianity is not just an optional act but rather a commandment. The Bible teaches that believers are to follow Christ's example in giving generously without seeking personal gain. The Apostle Paul writes about Generosity in his letters, emphasizing that it should come from a cheerful heart.

In the book of 2 Corinthians, Paul writes: *"Each one must give as he has decided in his heart, not reluctantly or under compulsion, for God loves a cheerful giver."* (2 Corinthians 9:7).

The Blessings of Generosity

Christianity teaches that Generosity brings blessings, both for the giver and the receiver. Giving is not only about helping others but also about growing spiritually. Christians believe that when they give, they are participating in God's work and spreading His love; it is believed that God blesses those who give selflessly, both in this life and in the life to come.

Jesus taught His followers that giving should not be done for the praise of others but rather as an act of love and devotion to God. In the Gospel of Matthew, He says: *"Give, and it will be given to you. A good measure, pressed down, shaken together, and running over, will be poured into your lap. For with the measure you use, it will be measured to you."* (Luke 6:38).

Generosity as a Reflection of God's Love

At the heart of Christian generosity is the belief that all generosity comes from God, the ultimate giver. Christians believe that God has given them life, grace, and salvation, and that, in turn, they are called to be generous to others. The ultimate act of generosity in

Christianity is the sacrifice of Jesus Christ on the cross, giving His life for the forgiveness of sins.

In the book of John, it is written: *"For God so loved the world that "He gave His one and only Son, that whoever believes in Him shall not perish but have eternal life."* (John 3:16).

The Biblical Call for Generosity and Church Donations

The Bible encourages generosity, though it doesn't specify precisely where donations should be directed. In Christian teachings, giving is viewed as a mean to further the church's mission, spread the gospel, and support those in need. Donating to the church is often seen as an act of faith, trusting that the funds will be used in alignment with Christian values—such as supporting ministries, missions, and charitable works. The Bible urges believers to support their local church community, which helps the poor, funds religious activities, and provides a place for worship and fellowship:

"Do not neglect to do good and to share what you have, for such sacrifices are pleasing to God." (Hebrews 13:16).

While giving to the church is seen as part of supporting the gospel, the use of funds must remain transparent, ethical, and consistent with Christian teachings. Church leaders, particularly those with significant wealth, must ensure their actions and lifestyles reflect the humility and service that Jesus exemplified. Ultimately, Christians are called to give out of love, not for material gain, and to support causes that uplift society—especially the poor, the needy, and the marginalized.

Church Donations and Their Use

Donations to churches serve various purposes, such as maintaining church buildings, paying staff (including pastors and administrative staff), funding outreach programs (like food banks and missionary work), and supporting charitable initiatives. Many churches also allocate funds for events and services that offer spiritual support to the community. For example, a portion of donations may be given to those in need—providing food, clothing, shelter, or assistance for the sick and poor. Some churches also contribute to local and international humanitarian efforts.

The Wealth of Church Leaders

While many church leaders live lives of humility and simplicity, certain high-ranking leaders have amassed considerable wealth, raising concerns within the congregation and the broader community about how funds are being used. Several factors contribute to this wealth:

> **Historical and cultural influences:** Church leaders in some traditions may have access to wealth or status due to their role in managing large congregations or church institutions.

Private donations: Wealthy benefactors may donate large sums to particular churches or religious leaders, increasing the financial resources available.

Personal lifestyle choices: Some religious leaders may lead affluent lifestyles that reflect personal wealth rather than church funds, which can conflict with Christian teachings of humility.

Challenges, Criticism, and Ethical Considerations

Church leaders' wealth accumulation and donation management can sometimes lead to criticism, particularly if funds are perceived to be misused or misaligned with Christian values of humility, poverty, and service. High-profile cases of church leaders living in luxury while their congregations struggle with poverty can create tensions and prompt calls for greater transparency and accountability in how donations are used.

Many Christians believe the church's or its leaders' wealth should be used ethically, benefiting the wider community. Churches that emphasize social justice, poverty alleviation, and aiding the marginalized are often seen as setting a good example for responsible donation use. These principles align with the Christian call to care for the poor, sick, and oppressed. In contrast, churches that prioritize accumulating wealth for leaders or the institution may be seen as not fully reflecting the teachings of Christ, who emphasized storing up treasures in heaven, not on earth (Matthew 6:19-21).

Transparency, Accountability, and Legal Framework

The issue of church leaders or institutions becoming wealthy from donations is complex and often influenced by different religious traditions, interpretations of scripture, and legal frameworks. While the wealth accumulated by church leaders raises ethical and moral questions, it's not always illegal due to the exemptions granted to religious organizations, particularly those with tax-exempt status in many countries. For example, in the United States, churches are exempt from specific regulations and public financial disclosures, making it difficult to track how donations are used.

Some church leaders argue that their wealth is a blessing from God or a result of their success in ministry. They may justify their lifestyle as a reflection of the abundance that comes from faithfulness. Others may use their wealth to fund additional ministries or outreach. Additionally, wealthy individuals may donate large sums to religious leaders or churches, resulting in more significant wealth for the leaders, even if the church itself is not benefiting directly from the donations.

While legal protections for religious freedom give churches and leaders significant autonomy, these exemptions often spark calls for greater financial transparency and accountability. Ethical concerns arise when there is a perceived discrepancy between Christ's teachings about humility and the lifestyles of some leaders. Many within the faith community advocate for reforms, including clearer guidelines on how donations should be used to ensure that funds are directed toward the church's mission and service to the poor rather than enriching church leaders.

GENEROSITY IN THE TORAH

Generosity is a fundamental value in the Torah, reflecting a person's piety and commitment to helping others, particularly those in need. As part of the Jewish Bible, the Torah emphasizes the importance of supporting the poor, the sick, and the marginalized. It presents generosity as a religious or ethical duty and an essential act of faith and social justice. Below are key principles of generosity in the Torah:

Caring for the Poor and Needy

The Torah commands care and support for those who are struggling due to poverty or hardship. In Deuteronomy 15:7-8, it states:

"If there is a poor man among you... Do not harden your heart or shut your hand off your poor brother. Rather, open your hand wide to him and willingly lend him sufficient for his need."

This highlights the immediate and compassionate response required to help those in need.

Tithing: A System of Structured Giving

Tithing—the practice of giving 10% of one's income—is a central concept in the Torah. The Israelites were commanded to set aside a tenth of their produce or earnings to support the Temple, the priests, and the Levites. It also served as a means of helping the poor. Deuteronomy 14:28-29 states:

"You shall surely tithe all the produce of your seed that the field brings forth year by year."

While the New Testament does not emphasize tithing in the same way, the principle of generous giving remains a core value in Jewish tradition.

The Virtue of Hospitality

Hospitality is highly valued in the Torah, encouraging kindness toward strangers and those in need. One of the most well-known examples is found in **Genesis 18:2**, where Abraham welcomes three strangers into his home:

"And he lifted his eyes and looked, and behold, three men were standing by him."

This act of generosity exemplifies the importance of opening one's home and heart to others, reinforcing the Torah's emphasis on kindness and care for all.

Generosity as an Act of Obedience to God

Giving is not merely an act of charity; it is an act of obedience to God. The Torah teaches that God blesses those who give generously. Proverbs 19:17 states:

"Whoever is generous to the poor lends to the Lord, and He will repay him for his deed."

This verse highlights the spiritual connection between generosity and divine blessing.

Mercy and Compassion for the Vulnerable

The Torah repeatedly stresses the importance of protecting and caring for the most vulnerable members of society, including widows and orphans. Exodus 22:22 warns:

"You shall not afflict any widow or orphan."

This command underscores the moral responsibility to show mercy and compassion, ensuring no one is left without support.

The Release of Debts in the Seventh Year (The Year of Jubilee)

The Torah mandates the forgiveness of debts every seven years, known as the Year of Jubilee. During this time, all debts were canceled, and land was returned to its original owners, providing a fresh start for those in financial distress. Leviticus 25:13 declares:

"In this Year of Jubilee, every man shall return to his possession."

This principle demonstrates that generosity is about giving, creating economic fairness, and preventing long-term poverty.

Generosity Through Land Stewardship

The Torah also encourages generosity in agricultural practices. Farmers were instructed to leave the corners of their fields unharvested so the poor could gather food. **Leviticus 23:22** states:

"When you reap the harvest of your land, you shall not reap to the very corners of your field, nor shall you gather the gleanings of your harvest."

This commandment reflects a broader understanding of generosity—not just in money or goods but in sharing resources to ensure no one goes hungry.

Generosity as a Principle of Social Justice

In the Torah, generosity is more than just an act of kindness; it is a fundamental aspect of social justice. God expresses profound concern for the poor and calls His people to act in ways that reflect this concern. Generosity promotes fairness and equality, ensuring that everyone, especially the most vulnerable—has the resources to thrive.

Tzedakah: The Jewish Concept of Charity

In Judaism, tzedakah (צדקה) goes beyond voluntary charity—it is a moral and religious duty. Jewish tradition places great emphasis on structured giving, ensuring that those in need receive support.

Helping the Poor – Jewish law encourages giving not only to fellow Jews but to all those in need.

Community Support – Many Jewish organizations provide financial aid for education, medical assistance, and basic necessities.

Mutual Aid – Historically, Jewish communities have established

communal funds, interest-free loan
societies (Gemach), and other support
systems to assist those facing hardship.

Through tzedakah, generosity becomes a way
to uphold justice, strengthen communities, and
fulfill religious obligations.

GENEROSITY IN ISLAM: PRINCIPLES AND RELIGIOUS LAW

THE CONCEPT OF GENEROSITY IN ISLAM

Generosity (al-Karam - الكرم) is one of the most emphasized virtues in Islam. It is seen as an essential characteristic of a true believer and a means of purifying one's wealth, soul, and character. Generosity in Islam is deeply connected to faith (Iman), as Allah describes the righteous as those who give freely, seeking His pleasure rather than worldly gain. This act of giving not only purifies one's wealth but also enriches the soul, strengthening the bond with Allah.

Allah says in The Qur'an:

"You will never attain righteousness until you spend from that which you love. And whatever you spend—indeed, Allah is Knowing of it." (Surah Aal-e-Imran 3:92)

The Prophet Muhammad (peace be upon him) was known as the most generous of people, especially during Ramadan. His generosity was described as being like a "swift, unrestrained wind" that brings benefit to everyone (Sahih Bukhari, 6).

Forms of Generosity in Islam

Generosity in Islam takes multiple forms, some obligatory and others voluntary but highly recommended.

Obligatory Generosity: Zakat (الزكاة)

Zakat is a fundamental pillar of Islam and a form of compulsory charity. It is a specific portion of wealth that every eligible Muslim must give to those in need.

Who must give Zakat?

Any Muslim whose wealth exceeds a certain threshold (**Nisab**) must pay 2.5% of their savings annually.

Who receives Zakat? (Surah At-Tawbah 9:60)

The needy (Al-Fuqara) refers to those who are extremely poor and lack necessities.

The needy (Al-Masakin) refers to those in need but may have some resources yet still struggle to meet their needs.

Those employed to distribute Zakat.

New Muslims who need support (Mu'allafatu Qulubuhum).

Those who enslave or capture others need to free them.

People in debt.

Those striving in the path of Allah (Fi Sabilillah).

Stranded travelers.

Zakat is not charity in the sense of optional giving—it is every eligible Muslim's duty to ensure wealth redistribution and reduce economic disparity.

Voluntary Generosity: Sadaqah (الصدقة)

Unlike Zakat, people can give Sadaqah as an optional act of charity at any time and at any amount. They can provide money, food, knowledge, kindness, and even a smile.

The Prophet Muhammad (peace be upon him) said:

"Every act of goodness is charity." (Sahih Muslim)

Different Types of Sadaqah

Sadaqah Maaliyah (Material Charity) – Donating money, food, clothes, or other possessions.

Sadaqah Jariyah (Continuous Charity) – Charity that continues to benefit people after one's death, such as:

Building a well

Establishing a school or mosque

Publishing beneficial knowledge

Sponsoring an orphan

Sadaqah in Deeds – Smiling, speaking good words, helping others.

Generosity in Hospitality

Islam places great emphasis on honoring guests and being generous in hospitality.

The Prophet Muhammad (peace be upon him) said:

"Whoever believes in Allah and the Last Day, let him honor his guest." (Sahih Bukhari)

In Arab culture, influenced by Islamic teachings, hospitality is a sacred duty, and feeding guests—especially travelers and people in need—is highly rewarded in Islam.

Waqf (Endowment for Public Benefit)

Waqf (الوقف) is a form of charity where wealth is donated for continuous public benefit. The wealth itself is preserved, while its benefits are used for good causes, such as:

Building schools, hospitals, and mosques.

Supporting students, widows, or orphans.

Historically, Waqf institutions played a significant role in education, healthcare, and welfare in Muslim societies, and many still function today. This rich heritage of generosity and public service is a source of pride for Muslims, reflecting the enduring values of their faith.

Generosity as a Religious Law in Islam

How Generosity Became a Religious Principle

The Qur'an – Generosity is emphasized throughout the Qur'an as a means of purification, righteousness, and success.

"And spend [in the way of Allah] from what We have provided you before death approaches one of you..." (Surah Al-Munafiqun 63:10)

The Sunnah (Prophetic Tradition) – The Prophet Muhammad (peace be upon him) was the most generous person and constantly encouraged generosity.

The Concept of Barakah (Blessing) – Islam teaches that giving does not decrease wealth but increases it spiritually and materially.

The Prophet said: *"Charity does not decrease wealth."* (Sahih Muslim)

Social Justice in Islam – Islam views generosity as a means to establish economic balance and protect society from greed and corruption.

Institutionalization of Generosity in Islamic Society

Over centuries, generosity in Islam became structured through:

The Zakat System – Many Muslim countries have government-administered Zakat funds to distribute charity.

Islamic Charitable Organizations – Today, organizations such as Islamic Relief and the Red Crescent provide disaster relief and aid worldwide.

Waqf Institutions – Waqf endowments fund many hospitals, universities, and orphanages.

GENEROSITY IN BUDDHISM: PRINCIPLES AND RELIGIOUS LAW

The Concept of Generosity in Buddhism

Generosity in Buddhism transcends mere ethical practice—it stands as the gateway to spiritual growth and enlightenment. Its significance is underscored by its position as the first of the Ten Pāramitās (Perfections) in Mahāyāna Buddhism and the Ten Dasa-Pāramīs in Theravāda Buddhism. In these traditions, Dāna (दान) is not just a virtue, but a foundational practice that emphasizes selflessness, detachment, and compassion, laying the groundwork for cultivating higher perfections such as morality (Śīla) and wisdom (Prajñā).

The transformative power of Dāna, placed as the foremost perfection, is truly inspiring. By practicing generosity, individuals condition their minds to release selfish desires, reducing attachment and fostering inner freedom. This mindset benefits personal spiritual development and nurtures harmonious relationships and a compassionate society.

Unlike religious traditions where charity may be seen as an obligation, generosity in Buddhism is considered an act of merit (puñña) that generates good karma and supports the journey toward enlightenment. It encompasses much more than material giving. Offering time, sharing wisdom, and even granting the gift of fearlessness (abhaya-dāna)—protecting others from harm—are all forms of Dāna.

Selfless giving is profoundly connected to detachment, as it helps practitioners overcome greed and attachment to possessions or personal gain. Through this practice, Buddhists cultivate a generous spirit that nurtures both their character and society's collective well-being, illuminating the path to liberation.

Forms of Generosity in Buddhism

Material Generosity (Āmisa-Dāna)

Giving material goods, such as food, clothing, money, and shelter.

This is commonly observed in offerings to monks and temples and charitable donations to people in need.

Dhamma Generosity (Dhamma-Dāna)

Sharing spiritual wisdom and teachings with others.

The Buddha regarded this as the highest form of giving, as it leads others toward enlightenment.

Monks, teachers, and lay practitioners engage in this by giving sermons, writing scriptures, and guiding students.

Generosity of Fearlessness (Abhaya-Dāna)

Protecting others from fear, harm, and suffering.

This can include rescuing beings from danger, advocating for justice, or offering emotional support and encouragement.

Kusala (Skillful Generosity)

Giving with the right intention—without expecting anything in return.

Acts of generosity should come from a pure heart rather than for social recognition or material rewards.

Sangha Dāna (Offering to Monks and Nuns)

Laypeople traditionally support the monastic community through daily alms (Pindapata).

In return, monks provide spiritual guidance and uphold Buddhist teachings.

Generosity as a Religious Law in Buddhism

Unlike Islam, where charity is legally structured (such as Zakat), generosity in Buddhism is not enforced by law but is deeply embedded in moral and spiritual practice. However, generosity is considered a social and ethical duty, and Buddhist communities have institutionalized forms of giving to ensure its continuation.

How Generosity Became a Religious Principle

Teachings of the Buddha

The Buddha repeatedly emphasized generosity as the foundation of a virtuous life. He stated:

"If beings knew, as I know, the results of giving and sharing, they would not eat without having given" (Itivuttaka 26).

Karma and Rebirth

Acts of generosity generate good karma, leading to favorable rebirths and progress toward Nirvana.

Jataka Tales

Many stories about the Buddha's past lives (Jataka tales) illustrate how he perfected generosity through countless lifetimes.

Generosity in Buddhist Monastic Life

Dāna plays a central role in the relationship between laypeople and the Sangha (monastic community), making each individual feel included and valued.

Lay followers give material support to monks, ensuring their survival.

Monks, in turn, offer spiritual teachings, preserving and spreading Buddhist wisdom.

Monastic rules prohibit monks from owning property or engaging in trade, making them entirely dependent on lay generosity.

Institutionalization of Generosity in Buddhism

Over time, Buddhist communities have formalized generosity through various means: Monasteries as charitable centers – Historically, monasteries provided food, shelter, and medicine to the people in need.

Endowments and temple funds – Many temples manage funds for community welfare projects.

Buddhist charity organizations – Modern Buddhist organizations, such as Tzu Chi (Taiwan), focus on disaster relief, education, and healthcare.

Modern Applications of Generosity in Buddhism

Kathina Ceremonies

In countries like Thailand, Sri Lanka, and Myanmar, Kathina ceremonies involve large-scale donations to monks.

Buddhist Humanitarian Efforts

Buddhist charities provide disaster relief, education, and healthcare worldwide.

Engaged Buddhism

Founded by Thich Nhat Hanh, Engaged Buddhism promotes generosity in social activism and humanitarian work.

In the Abrahamic religions—Islam, Christianity, and Judaism—generosity is deeply connected to God's will and divine reward. Giving is not just an act of obedience to God, but a profound reflection of His mercy, and a path to receiving His blessings. Each faith emphasizes generosity as a fundamental moral and spiritual duty, a responsibility that carries significant weight:

> Islam views generosity (*Zakat* and *Sadaqah*) as a means of purifying wealth and earning divine rewards. Giving is a religious obligation that promotes social justice and strengthens faith.

> Christianity teaches that generosity mirrors God's grace. Selfless giving is an expression of faith and is seen as storing up "treasures in heaven."

> Judaism upholds *Tzedakah* as an act of righteousness and justice. It is more

than charity—it is a moral duty that aligns one with God's will.

In contrast, Buddhism approaches generosity (*Dāna*) from a personal and philosophical perspective, focusing on self-transformation rather than divine command. Giving is not about pleasing a deity but about cultivating selflessness and detachment from material possessions. The act of generosity in Buddhism is a powerful tool for personal growth, generating good karma and helping one progress toward enlightenment by reducing greed and attachment.

Thus, while generosity in the Abrahamic traditions is primarily an act of divine obedience, moral duty, and spiritual reward, in Buddhism, it is a practice of personal growth, detachment, and inner peace.

Generosity, whether rooted in divine obedience or personal growth, is not a negative form of giving. When done sincerely and ethically, it serves a vital role in helping those in need and

uplifting individuals from hardship to stability.
The motivations may differ—whether seeking
divine reward, fulfilling a moral duty, or
cultivating inner peace—but the impact
remains universally positive.

When generosity is not directed toward a
specific person for personal gain but rather
aimed at addressing real needs in society, it
becomes a force for good. It provides essential
support, fosters social justice, and helps
individuals move from a place of struggle to a
place of security. Done right, it is an expression
of compassion and responsibility that
strengthens both communities and individuals.

Cultural Expectations and Generosity

Cultural norms also play a significant role in
shaping attitudes toward generosity,
influencing how, when, and to whom
individuals give. These norms are often
influenced by power dynamics within a society,
with those in positions of authority or privilege

often setting the expectations for generosity. In many societies, generosity is closely tied to concepts of honor, reputation, and social cohesion, often leading to behaviors that reflect both positive and problematic dynamics.

Generosity as a Marker of Social Status

In numerous cultures, acts of giving are associated with social prestige and recognition. Wealthy individuals or families may engage in conspicuous displays of generosity—such as funding public works, hosting lavish events, or making grand charitable donations—as a way of affirming their status within the community. While these acts can benefit society, they may also perpetuate a cycle of competition, where generosity becomes less about altruism and more about maintaining or enhancing one's reputation.

For example:

> In some South Asian cultures, families hosting weddings or religious

celebrations may feel compelled to provide extravagant feasts and gifts to guests, driven by the fear of social judgment. This form of material generosity, while rooted in cultural tradition, can lead to financial hardship or perpetuate a culture of comparison and excess.

In certain Indigenous communities, traditions like the potlatch ceremony involve redistributing wealth as a means of demonstrating leadership and community support. While the practice is intended to foster equality, it can also create social tension or rivalry when interpreted through a competitive lens.

Gendered Expectations of Generosity

Cultural norms often dictate different expectations for men and women in acts of generosity. Women, for example, may be socialized to prioritize emotional and caregiving forms of generosity, such as nurturing family members, volunteering in the community, or offering emotional support. Men, on the other hand, may be encouraged to demonstrate their generosity through financial provision or public acts of charity.

These gendered expectations can lead to unequal burdens and unrecognized contributions:

> Women may feel obligated to sacrifice their time, energy, and emotional well-being to meet the needs of others, often at the expense of their own self-care or aspirations.

> Men may experience pressure to be the primary providers in their families, leading to overwork, financial strain, or feelings of inadequacy if they are unable to meet societal standards of generosity.

Generosity in the Age of Globalization

In today's interconnected world, cultural and religious influences on generosity are increasingly intertwined with global trends and challenges. Migration, diaspora communities, and cross-cultural exchange have broadened the practice and understanding of generosity. This global context has led to the emergence of hybrid expressions of generosity and the inspiration of global-scale generosity through diverse cultural and religious narratives.

> Diaspora communities may maintain traditional giving practices while also adapting to the norms of their host countries, creating hybrid expressions of generosity.

> Global fundraising campaigns, such as those for disaster relief or humanitarian crises, draw on diverse cultural and religious narratives to inspire generosity on a global scale.

However, globalization also highlights the disparities and contradictions in how generosity is perceived and practiced across different cultural and religious contexts.

Performative Generosity: When Generosity is Driven by the Desire for Social Recognition: When generosity is motivated by the desire for social recognition or approval, it can become performative rather than authentic. For example, individuals or organizations may engage in charitable acts primarily to enhance their public image rather than out of genuine concern for others. This can be seen in the case of corporate social responsibility initiatives that are more about marketing than social impact, or in the behavior of individuals who make a show of their charitable acts on social media.

Exploitation of Vulnerability

Religious institutions, cultural leaders, or community organizations may exploit individuals' sense of duty or faith to solicit donations or labor. This exploitation can erode trust and create long-lasting harm, particularly when vulnerable populations are targeted, underscoring the need for ethical considerations in generosity practices.

THE BAD LUCK OF PATHOLOGICAL GENEROSITY

Generosity, when practiced wisely and intentionally, nurtures fulfillment and joy. However, when generosity becomes pathological — driven by fear, guilt, or the compulsion to gain approval — it disrupts the giver's internal state, creating an energetic imbalance. This disruption often leads to bad luck, not because of some external force, but because the giver unconsciously locks themselves into a role where they only give without ever receiving.

This self-imposed energetic loop leads to emotional exhaustion, resentment, and missed opportunities. The giver may become blind to chances for abundance or even repel positive outcomes because they have mentally conditioned themselves to be only in the energy of giving. When one operates solely in the giving frequency, receiving becomes impossible — which is essentially the true nature of bad luck.

The Mirage of Pathological Generosity and the Bad Luck It Brings

Pathological generosity traps individuals in a deceptive pursuit, much like chasing a desert mirage. Endless giving appears to promise love, approval, or success. Yet, the anticipated exchange never materializes. Instead, the giver is left drained, disillusioned, and ensnared in a relentless cycle of giving without reciprocation.

This pattern often breeds inner frustration and a sense of misfortune, as the giver repeatedly invests time, energy, emotions, material resources, or intimacy, only to receive little or nothing of true value in return. Clinging to the hope that the next act of generosity will finally unlock the validation they crave, they find themselves perpetually disappointed.

How Pathological Generosity Becomes a Mirage

Material Generosity:

Givers endlessly support others financially, hoping for loyalty or gratitude, only to find themselves abandoned or taken advantage of when their resources run dry.

Emotional Generosity:

They pour emotional energy into others, believing it will forge deeper connections, but they often end up being the emotional dumpground with no reciprocation.

Time and Energy Generosity:

By prioritizing others' needs over their own, they chase the false promise that sacrifice will bring respect or recognition, yet their efforts often go unnoticed or unappreciated.

Intellectual Generosity:

Sharing ideas freely without boundaries may seem noble, but when those ideas are taken without acknowledgment, the giver feels exploited and disillusioned.

Intimacy Generosity:

Offering trust and vulnerability too quickly, expecting authentic connection in return, often results in betrayal or indifference instead of meaningful bonds.

The Curse of Chasing the Mirage

The bad luck stemming from pathological generosity lies in its inherent imbalance. The giver becomes trapped in the energy of output, subconsciously reinforcing a mindset where receiving seems impossible. They are so focused on giving that they lose sight of their own worth and needs, making it nearly Impossible to attract healthy relationships, success, or happiness.

This imbalance leads to a self-fulfilling prophecy: the more they chase validation through giving, the less they receive, reinforcing the false belief that they must give even more to be valued. They remain stuck in a desert, forever pursuing a mirage that disappears with every step forward.

Breaking Free from the Mirage

To reclaim their power and restore balance, individuals must recognize that healthy giving is reciprocal, intentional, and aligned with personal well-being.

Stop Chasing. Acknowledge that endless giving will never yield the desired result, especially when the need for external validation drives it.

Embrace Reciprocity: Cultivate relationships where both giving and receiving are natural and balanced.

Set Boundaries: Protect personal resources by setting clear limits on what to offer and when.

Redefine Generosity: Shift from compulsive giving to intentional contributions from an abundance mindset rather than emptiness.

The Five Forms of Pathological Generosity and Their Consequences

Material Generosity:

Even when it causes financial harm, overgiving money or possessions often stems from a desire to gain approval or prove worthiness.

> **Consequence:** The giver may face persistent financial instability and attract those who exploit their resources. Instead of prosperity, they experience continuous financial setbacks and hardships.

Emotional Generosity:

Offering endless emotional support without setting boundaries, often out of fear of rejection or alienation.

> **Consequence:** Emotional over-givers frequently attract emotionally needy individuals

who drain their energy. They may feel depleted, unsupported, and resentful, creating internal chaos that blocks emotional fulfillment.

Time and Energy Generosity:

Giving away too much time and energy to others at the expense of personal priorities and goals.

Consequence: Over time, this leads to chronic stress, lost personal opportunities, and burnout. The giver may feel stuck in a cycle of endless obligations while achieving little personal progress.

Intellectual Generosity:

Sharing valuable insights, knowledge, or creative ideas without boundaries, often to gain recognition or approval.

Consequence: The giver's contributions may be exploited

without acknowledgment or not
be respected for giving
unsolicited information, leading to
frustration, diminished
confidence, and a sense of
intellectual depletion.

Intimacy Generosity:

Offering trust and vulnerability too freely,
even when the other person has not
earned it or proven trustworthy.

> **Consequence:** This can result in
> betrayal, emotional wounds, a
> loss of self-respect, and a run of
> reputation, which can be
> detrimental to good luck. The
> giver may find themselves unable
> to form meaningful connections
> due to repeated emotional harm.

The Energetic Imbalance and Self-Created Bad Luck

When generosity becomes pathological, the giver conditions themselves to exist solely in a state of output—always offering but never expecting or allowing themselves to receive. This mental programming fosters a life experience where opportunities for abundance, joy, or meaningful connections are blocked. The giver becomes out of sync with their own needs and blind to moments when they could benefit or be uplifted by others.

This self-inflicted imbalance manifests as bad luck. The giver may wonder why nothing ever goes their way, why relationships feel one-sided, or why success remains elusive. In reality, they have trained their subconscious mind to perceive receiving as unnecessary or selfish, locking themselves in a perpetual depletion state.

Restoring Balance and Reclaiming Good Luck

Recognize the Pattern:

Awareness is the first step to breaking the cycle. Identify areas where giving has become compulsive, draining, or transactional.

Set Clear Boundaries:

Protect personal energy by setting limits on how much to give, whether in material goods, time, or emotional support.

Embrace the Art of Receiving:

Intentionally practice receiving without guilt. Accept compliments, assistance, and support as natural parts of balanced relationships.

Reprogram Beliefs Around Generosity:

Shift from a belief that giving equals worthiness to understanding that healthy relationships and success require reciprocity.

Prioritize Self-Preservation:

Retain energy for personal growth and fulfillment. Generosity should come from a place of abundance, not compulsion or fear.

By restoring balance, individuals can break free from self-created misfortune and transform their generosity into a meaningful, empowering, and fulfilling force—pathological giving drains balanced giving uplifts. True abundance and good fortune emerge when the illusion of the mirage is shattered, revealing that healthy generosity is rooted in balance—not endless sacrifices. Giving becomes a source of joy with this shift, and life's genuine rewards naturally follow.

BREAKING THE CYCLE OF TOXIC GENEROSITY

Generosity is often seen as a virtue that strengthens bonds, deepens relationships, and creates a sense of purpose. However, giving is rare without expectation. Consciously or unconsciously, people often give with the hope of receiving something in return—gratitude, respect, emotional support, or a future favor. While reciprocity is a natural part of human relationships, unchecked generosity can become a source of imbalance, leading to exhaustion, exploitation, and unfulfilled expectations.

Even acts of giving done in secrecy are not always entirely selfless. Many offer charity in hopes of divine reward, seeking spiritual merit or favor in the afterlife. While noble, this form of generosity is still shaped by the desire for something in return—albeit from God rather than people. True selflessness, free from any expectation of reciprocation, is rare. It exists when giving stems purely from kindness, with no hope of acknowledgment, social validation, or spiritual gain. In this sense, those who do not seek divine reward or recognition may sometimes be the most selfless, giving with no expectation of return from anyone or anything.

The Lesson of Unprotected Energy and Resources

A well-known Arabic proverb states: " المال السائب يعلّم السرقة"—"Unattended money teaches theft." This wisdom serves as a powerful metaphor, illustrating that anything valuable—whether wealth, time, emotions, intellect, or intimacy—when given indiscriminately or for misguided reasons, not only risks being misused but can also bring harm to the giver. Contrary to the belief that all acts of giving will be met with divine reward, this Proverb warns against the dangers of unchecked generosity. Many ancient traditions across cultures echo this caution, emphasizing the importance of wise stewardship and self-protection.

Throughout history, various cultures and traditions have imparted wisdom about the dangers of excessive, unreciprocated generosity and the necessity of boundaries:

> **Jewish Wisdom (Pirkei Avot):** "Build a fence around the Torah' teaches that even sacred things require protection to prevent misuse. Just as religious knowledge must be safeguarded, so too must our emotional and mental well-being be protected through boundaries.
>
> **Islamic Teaching (Hadith):** *"Tie your camel and trust in Allah."* This wisdom from Prophet Muhammad (peace be upon him) highlights the balance between faith and responsibility. One must take practical steps to safeguard what is valuable before relying on divine intervention.

Hindu Wisdom (Bhagavad Gita): *"A man's self is his friend. A man's self is his foe."* Over-giving without self-care turns us into our own worst enemy. True generosity must include kindness to ourselves, ensuring we do not deplete our well-being in the service of others.

Chinese Proverb: *"Do not blame the thief; blame the one who leaves the door open."* This underscores personal accountability. If we give indiscriminately and fail to set limits, we invite exploitation. Our responsibility is to protect our resources—emotional, physical, or financial—.

African Proverb: *"If there is no enemy within, the enemy outside can do you no harm."* This reminds us that overextending ourselves weakens our inner strength, making us more vulnerable to external exploitation.

Protecting our energy allows us to remain resilient.

Native American (Lakota) Proverb: *"Force, no matter how concealed, begets resistance."* Giving should come from genuine willingness, not guilt or pressure. When generosity is forced, whether by societal expectations or personal guilt—it breeds resentment and emotional exhaustion.

Ancient Greek Proverb: *"Nothing in excess."* Even virtues like kindness and generosity become harmful when taken to an extreme. Balance is key to sustainable giving.

Taoist Wisdom (Tao Te Ching): *"He who knows that enough is enough will always have enough."* Over-giving leads to depletion while knowing when to stop ensures sustainability in both life and relationships.

English Proverb: *"Possession is nine-tenths of the law."* Simply having something doesn't mean it's secure—without proper stewardship, it can be lost or taken. The same applies to emotional energy, time, and resources; if not properly managed, others can deplete them.

Persian Proverb: *"A fool may throw a stone into a well which a hundred wise men cannot pull out."* Careless or excessive generosity can create damage that is difficult to undo. Thoughtful giving prevents regret.

Russian Proverb: *"A kind-hearted fool gets eaten by the wolves."* Kindness without wisdom invites exploitation. Generosity must be paired with discernment to avoid becoming prey to those who take advantage.

Filipino Proverb: *"Do not give more than what your hands can hold."*

Overextending oneself leads to personal depletion, making it impossible to continue giving healthily. Sustainable generosity requires limits.

Brazilian Proverb: *"The candle that burns too bright burns out quickly."* Excessive generosity can lead to exhaustion and suffering. True kindness must be sustainable, ensuring that the giver does not burn out in the process.

Sufi Wisdom states, *"The one who does not guard his heart will lose his soul."* If we give away too much of our emotional energy without protection, we risk losing our sense of self. Protecting our hearts is an act of wisdom, not selfishness.

Reclaiming Balanced Giving

Recognizing the dangers of unguarded generosity through self-awareness and a self-sufficient ego is only the beginning. True healing lies in reclaiming agency, discernment, and balance—transforming generosity from a source of depletion into a wellspring of strength.

The Path to Healing:

Reclaiming Balanced Generosity

Restoring Balanced Generosity

Recognizing the dangers of unchecked generosity through self-awareness and a stable sense of self is only the beginning. True healing lies in reclaiming control, practicing discernment, and achieving balance—transforming generosity from a source of depletion into a wellspring of strength.

The Path to Healing: Restoring Balanced Generosity

Discernment: Knowing When and Where to Give

Generosity should not be automatic, driven by guilt, or fueled by ego. Instead, it must be intentional and rooted in wisdom. Before giving, ask yourself:

> Am I giving from abundance, or at the expense of my own well-being?

> Does this person or situation truly deserve my generosity, or am I reinforcing an imbalance?

> Is this act driven by conscious love, or is it an unbalanced impulse rooted in a sense of obligation to something beyond my responsibility?

> Am I giving from abundance, or am I sacrificing my own well-being?

Is this person or situation deserving of my generosity, or am I enabling imbalance?

True generosity is not about quantity but about quality and intention. Key considerations include:

Does my giving genuinely help the recipient, or is it driven by guilt or insecurity?

Am I giving from a place of abundance, or am I depleting myself in the process?

Does my generosity empower others, or does it create dependency?

By applying discernment, generosity shifts from reckless depletion to purposeful giving—one that nurtures rather than drains.

Reciprocity: The Art of Balanced Exchange

Healthy generosity is a two-way street. While true kindness expects nothing in return, sustainable giving must flow in both directions—even if not in the same form.

> Pay attention to patterns of take-and-take relationships.

> Invest in people and causes that appreciate and respect your contributions.

> Remember: A genuine relationship honors both giving and receiving.

Reciprocity isn't about keeping score, it's about fostering mutual respect, appreciation, and the exchange of energy.

Boundaries: The Guardian of Your Energy

Just as a dam controls the flow of water, boundaries regulate where your energy, time, and resources go. Without them, generosity turns into self-sacrifice.

> **Say no without guilt.** Declining is not selfish—it's an act of self-preservation.

> **Limit access to your time, emotions**, and intellect. Not everyone deserves full access to your generosity.

> **Pause before giving.** If giving has become an automatic reflex, stop and reassess.

Self-Worth: Valuing Yourself as Much as Others

A common belief lies at the root of pathological generosity: *"My worth is tied to what I give."* Healing means recognizing that your value exists beyond your sacrifices.

> **Give to yourself first.** You cannot pour from an empty cup. Prioritize rest, joy, and personal fulfillment.

Detach from external validation.
Detach from external validation. Your
worth is not defined by how much you
give. Let go of the need to be labeled as
the most generous, the most kind, or
any other title driven by ego.

Allow yourself to receive. Accept help,
love, and kindness without guilt—it is
not a sign of weakness but of balance.

Redefining Generosity: From Obligation to Choice

True healing is not about stopping generosity
but transforming it into something sustainable
and joyful.

Generosity should be a choice, not a
compulsion.

Healthy giving comes from fullness, not
emptiness.

When generosity is wise, it enriches
both the giver and the receiver.

Strategies for Breaking the Cycle:
Develop Self-Awareness

Understanding the root causes of excessive giving is the first step toward healing. Ask yourself:

> Why do I feel the need to give so much?
>
> Is my giving motivated by fear, insecurity, or a need for approval?
>
> How do I feel when I resist the urge to give?

Keeping a journal or seeking guidance from trusted mentors or therapists can help uncover unhealthy giving patterns.

Set Healthy Boundaries

Boundaries are essential for protecting emotional well-being and preventing burnout.

Practical Steps:

> Define clear limits on how much and how often you give.
>
> Practice saying "no" without guilt or excessive justification.
>
> Avoid over-explaining decisions when declining requests.

Example: Instead of constantly dropping everything to help a friend with minor problems, set reasonable limits and encourage their independence.

Redefine generosity

Shifting from compulsive to conscious generosity ensures that acts of kindness are enriching rather than draining.

Address the Fear of Alienation

Excessive giving is often rooted in a fear of rejection. Breaking free from this fear requires a shift in mindset:

Build self-worth independently of external validation.

Cultivate relationships based on mutual respect and energy exchange.

Challenge the belief that love, or acceptance is contingent on constant sacrifice.

Practice Self-Compassion

Self-compassion reduces the need to over-give as a means of proving self-worth.

Practical Steps:

Engage in mindfulness exercises to stay present and grounded.

Use positive affirmations to reinforce self-worth.

Recognize that prioritizing personal needs is essential for long-term well-being.

Seek Professional Guidance

For deeply ingrained patterns of toxic generosity, therapy or coaching can provide valuable tools and insights to help reshape unhealthy giving behaviors.

Emotional Energy: Constantly giving without limits can lead to exhaustion and manipulation.

Intellectual Energy: Sharing valuable ideas without discretion can result in stolen credit or misuse.

Time and Physical Energy: Always being available without setting boundaries can cause burnout and resentment.

Lessons for Personal Growth:

Establish Boundaries: Just as a locked treasure chest protects valuables, setting limits on emotional and intellectual investments preserves well-being.

Mindful Generosity: Giving should be intentional, not driven by guilt or compulsion.

Accountability: Recognizing personal responsibility in setting limits helps maintain balance in relationships.

By embracing discernment, reciprocity, boundaries, self-worth, and conscious choice, we reclaim a healthy form of generosity—one that heals rather than depletes. Breaking the cycle of toxic generosity leads to deeper, more fulfilling relationships and a more balanced approach to giving. When generosity arises from self-respect instead of compulsion, it transforms into a true act of kindness that enriches both the giver and the recipient.

Through cultivating self-awareness, setting firm boundaries, and practicing intentional generosity, we turn giving into a powerful force for connection rather than depletion. True generosity is not about sacrificing oneself for others but about sharing from a place of strength, wisdom, and authenticity. In this way, we create a healthier and more harmonious dynamic in our relationships and lives.

REFERENCES

Psychological and Behavioral Studies

Oakley, B., Knafo, A., Madhavan, G., & Wilson, D. S. (2012). *Pathological Altruism*. Oxford University Press.

Crocker, J., & Park, L. E. (2004). The Costly Pursuit of Self-Esteem: Implications for Self-Regulation. *Psychological Bulletin, 130(3)*, 392-414.

Zahn-Waxler, C., & Robinson, J. (1995). Mood and Parenting Influences on Social Development: Implications for the Development of Altruism and Empathy. In J. D. Osofsky (Ed.), *Handbook of Child Development* (2nd ed., pp. 401-426). Wiley.

Schwartz, J. E., & Rachlin, H. (2004). The Altruistic Personality: A Review of Psychological Literature. *Psychological Bulletin, 130(4)*, 507-528.

Figley, C. R. (1995). *Compassion Fatigue: Coping with Secondary Traumatic Stress Disorder in Those Who Treat the Traumatized*. Brunner/Mazel.

Strohme, J. L. A. H., et al. (2016). Burnout and Compassion Fatigue: The Role of

Empathy. *Journal of Mental Health Counseling,
38(2),* 140-155.

Bowlby, J. (1969). *Attachment and Loss: Volume
1. Attachment.* Basic Books.

Gergen, C. J., McGoldrick, M., & We, M. A.
(2016). Generosity and Over-Giving: The
Emotional and Psychological Costs of
Caretaking Roles. *Journal of Social and Personal
Relationships, 33(3),* 451-467.

Religions

Christianity

Gunther, W. T. (2016). *Theology and Ethics in
the New Testament: The Role of Generosity in Early
Christian Life.* Princeton University.

Chilton, B., & Linz, M. (Eds.).
(2017). *Generosity in the Bible: Theological
Reflections on Giving.* Oxford University Press.

Wright, N. T. (2014). *The New Testament and the
Mission of the Church.* Baker Academic Press.

Carter, W. R. (2018). *Christian Generosity in
Practice: A Study on Church Donations and Their
Uses.* Cambridge University.

Martin, J. L. (2015). *Paul and the Generosity of
Christ: Reflections on Christian Giving and the
Poor.* Fortress Press.

The Bible (King James Version):

Matthew 6:3-4.

Luke 6:38.

Judaism (Torah)

Friedman, L. (2002). *Generosity in the Torah: Biblical Foundations for Contemporary Giving.* Jewish Publication Society.

Hirsch, I. (2001). *The Ethics of the Torah: Charity, Justice, and Generosity in Jewish Tradition.* Ktav Publishing House.

Sarna, N. M. (1993). *The JPS Torah Commentary: Genesis.* Jewish Publication Society.

The Bible (King James Version):
Deuteronomy 15:7-8.

Islam

Qaradawi, Y. (1999). *Fiqh al-Zakat: A Comparative Study of Zakat, Its Philosophy, and Impact on Economics.* Islamic Foundation.

The Holy Qur'an:

Surah Al-Imran, 3:92.

Surah At-Tawbah, 9:60.

Surah Al-Munafiqun, 63:10.

Generosity in Buddhism

Bodhi, B. (2011). *The Buddha's Path to Deliverance*. Wisdom Publications.

Dhammapada: Sayings of the Buddha (Translation by Eknath Easwaran).

Medical and Mental Health Studies

University of Nebraska Medical Center. (2002). Study Investigating Whether Feeling Powerless in Relationships Leads to Self-Neglect of Health. University of Nebraska Medical Center.

Psychiatric Research. (n.d.). Imbalance in Daily Life and Overcommitment Can Predict Reduced Functionality. *PMC.NCBI.NLM.NIH.GOV*.

FINAL THOUGHTS

In the grand scheme of life, as we journey on this earth, we come to realize that true generosity is not about giving to the point of exhaustion or seeking external validation. It's about adopting a balanced and mindful approach, being generous to the body and nourishing the soul before extending that generosity to others. When generosity stems from inner strength and clarity, it nourishes both the giver and those around them. This perspective underscores the importance of protecting our mental and physical well-being through healthy boundaries, giving with discernment, and embracing kindness that is rooted in balanced awareness and sound reasoning. Striving for a life where generosity becomes a source of strength, nourishment, and growth fosters deeper, more meaningful relationships, leading to a profound sense of fulfillment for both the giver and the receiver.

.

ABOUT THE AUTHOR

Amy Law is a dedicated writer and author passionate about personal transformation and empowerment. Her work focuses on overcoming toxic influences that hinder growth and development, providing deep insights into the emotional and psychological impacts of unhealthy dynamics. With a keen understanding of human behavior, Amy offers practical tools to regain strength, set healthy boundaries, and achieve a balanced life.

Her writing blends wisdom with actionable strategies, helping readers navigate complex relationships and reclaim their personal and emotional independence. Through her compassionate and engaging style, Amy inspires others to confront challenges, break free from limiting patterns, and embrace their full potential.

www.ingramcontent.com/pod-product-compliance
Lightning Source LLC
Chambersburg PA
CBHW051510120626
46551CB00012B/860

* 9 7 9 8 9 9 1 4 1 7 1 0 5 *